UNDERSTANDING

EQUINE NEUROLOGICAL DISORDERS

YOUR **GUIDE** TO HORSE HEALTH
CARE AND MANAGEMENT

UNDERSTANDING

EQUINE NEUROLOGICAL DISORDERS

YOUR **GUIDE** TO HORSE HEALTH CARE AND MANAGEMENT

By Bradford G. Bentz, VMD, MS

Foreword by David E. Granstrom, DVM, PhD

The Blood-Horse, Inc. Lexington, KY

Other titles offered by
The Horse Health Care Library

Understanding EPM

Understanding Equine Lameness

Understanding Equine First Aid

Understanding the Equine Foot

Understanding Equine Nutrition

Understanding Laminitis

Understanding the Foal

Understanding the Broodmare

Understanding Basic Horse Care

Understanding the Stallion

Understanding Horse Behavior

Understanding Breeding Management

Understanding the Older Horse

Understanding Equine Law

Understanding the Young Horse

Understanding the Equine Eye

Understanding the Pony

The New Equine Sports Therapy

Horse Theft Prevention Handbook

Contents

FOREWORD

Equine neurologic disease often results in devastating consequences for horses and those who care for them. Unfortunately, neurologic disease is unusually complex and often difficult to understand. Noted equine internist Dr. Brad Bentz has prepared an extensive and balanced review of equine neurologic disease in an easy to understand format. He has drawn from many years of experience in private and university practice, as well as research he conducted at the University of Kentucky.

Dr. Bentz has included excellent background information that will help owners and caregivers understand the disease process and promote optimal communication with attending veterinarians. Information regarding specific diseases is presented clearly and conveniently in chapters based on underlying cause, e.g., trauma, infection, genetic or metabolic dysfunction.

The more those responsible for providing nursing care for horses know about the disease process, including treatment and recovery, the greater the chances for a positive outcome. Dr. Bentz has provided an excellent ready reference that should prove to be extremely valuable for years to come to everyone that cares for horses.

David E. Granstrom, DVM, PhD
Assistant Director
Education and Research Division
American Veterinary Medical Association

INTRODUCTION

Although nervous system disorders are seen with relative frequency in equine veterinary practice, they are less commonly encountered than a number of more common conditions that may affect a horse's gait. The classification of a horse as "neurologic" based on physical and neurologic examinations is a subjective assessment and may vary from one clinician to another.

Because of the highly subjective nature of the equine nervous system evaluation, particularly as it relates to gait, a number of horses without nervous system disease may be assessed with it, while others that may be neurologic may go undiagnosed. The addition of specific diagnostic tests, such as spinal fluid analysis and spinal X-rays, helps remove some of the subjectivity from the nervous system examination. Yet even many of the more specific tests have their limitations and may also be subject to "interpretation" that fails to produce a "black or white" answer.

The dissemination of information relating to equine nervous system disorders has been increased to a significant extent in the past several years. Much of this has followed a growing concern over the disease known as equine protozoal myeloencephalitis (EPM). Although it is usually beneficial to have information distributed, not all of the information pertaining to this disease or to the general understanding of equine neurology has been helpful. In some cases, it may even be misleading to the equine industry and its members.

I have had a keen interest in equine neurology since my internal medicine residency at the University of Pennsylvania's New Bolton Center. It was there where I was fortunate enough to have had Dr. Jill Beech as a mentor, who, perhaps without knowing, passed her interest, curiosity, and passion for equine neurology to me. In the early days of my interest, I became readily aware of the difficulties and misconceptions that prevailed over equine neurology. I have tried to help clarify the structure, function, and some disease processes for the layperson in this book.

Bradford G. Bentz, VMD, MS
Richmond, Kentucky

CHAPTER 1

Overview of the Equine Nervous System

The equine nervous system is essentially the same system that exists in all mammals, including humans. A useful way to think of its function and its physical makeup is to draw some parallels between the nervous system and an electrical system; this is because the nervous system func-

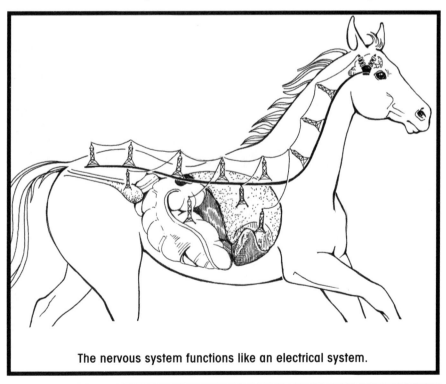

The nervous system functions like an electrical system.

tions on electrical impulses and currents at the cellular level.

At the center of the function of the nervous system is the central nervous system, which is comprised of the brain and the spinal cord. To use a simplified analogy, the brain is like the power company that supplies an entire region of homes with electricity. The individual homes are then analogous to those organs in the body that receive electrical impulses from the brain. Electrical impulses leave the power company via one very large wire, from which branches extend to individual homes. This large wire is like the spinal cord, and its branches are equivalent to the nerves that extend from the spinal cord.

AT A GLANCE

- The central nervous system consists of the brain and the spinal cord.

- The nerves that branch out from the spinal cord comprise the peripheral nervous system.

- The peripheral nervous system supplies electrical signals to the body's organs.

The nerves that branch out from the spinal cord comprise a second part of the nervous system, called the peripheral nervous system. The peripheral nervous system supplies "electrical signals" (nerve impulses) to the individual "homes" (organs). In any home (organ), there are various appliances, outlets, and electric lights that serve specific functions to make the home work as a whole. To continue the analogy, these appliances, outlets, and light fixtures are like the cells of the organ that require electrical impulses to perform certain functions as part of the whole organ.

The brain generates these electrical impulses from specific areas that are designated as the "control centers" of certain organs or subsets of organs. These electrical impulses are themselves generated from other, usually deeper, areas of the brain. The impulses may be generated voluntarily (the conscious decision to produce an effect, such as to move an arm or a leg) or involuntarily (without conscious effort; examples are blood-pressure control, heart rate, intestinal movement, etc.).

Regardless of how these electrical impulses are generated, they must be conducted to their target organs by nerves. This conduction takes place either through the spinal cord — or, in a few cases, via specialized nerves — directly from the brain or the brainstem (the uppermost part of the spinal cord that attaches the brain to the spinal cord) and to the peripheral nervous system. The peripheral nerves then carry these impulses to the target organs and cells.

The voluntary nervous system, also known as the somatic nervous system, is the part of the nervous system that carries consciously generated nerve impulses for consciously generated movements and effects. The involuntary nervous system, also called the autonomic nervous system, carries nerve impulses that are unconsciously or automatically generated. The autonomic nervous system is divided into two parts: the sympathetic (fight-or-flight responses) and the parasympathetic (generally opposite to sympathetic in function).

The horse's peripheral nervous system comprises seven cervical, 17 thoracic (chest), six lumbar, and four sacral nerves on each side of the body. As is the case in all mammals, 12 specialized nerves exit directly from the brain or the brainstem. These nerves are called the cranial nerves and are numbered I through XII according to where they exit the central nervous system. Many of these nerves carry fibers of the somatic and autonomic nervous system, and many also have "specialized" fibers associated with the special senses (taste, smell, vision, hearing, etc.).

The peripheral nervous system can be thought of as having two types of fibers within the nerves. The first, called motor fibers, initiate movement or cause an effect in the organ, tissue, or cell that is receiving the nerve input. The second, called sensory fiber, takes information from the organ, tissue, or cell and sends it back to the central nervous system for conscious or unconscious interpretation. The sensations of sight, touch or pain, hunger pangs, and hearing a noise are examples of information interpreted consciously; while information sent to the brain regarding blood pressure and heart rate are examples of information interpreted unconsciously.

CHAPTER 2

The Neurological Examination

Because animals cannot verbalize their sensations or feelings, evaluating their nervous systems is more difficult and subjective than it is in human medicine. However, certain types of responses and movements often are highly suggestive of nervous-system abnormalities. Furthermore, the manifestations of the failure of a certain organ or tissue function may also point toward nervous-system problems. The latter is especially true when this loss of function is diagnosed along with other clinical signs that indicate nervous derangement.

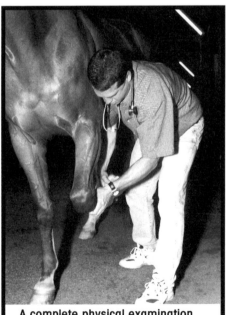

A complete physical examination...

Many reflex tests that are useful in diagnosing small animals are not practical for horses because of their size and general intolerance of unusual sensations, positions, and other challenges. For instance, a small-animal veterinarian can place a dog on its side to test the patellar reflex (the "knee-jerk reaction"); an equine veterinarian cannot do the same with his or her patients.

The neurologic examination should always begin with a good history and a complete general physical examination. History should include complaints and problems that have been noted with the horse. Attention to the signalment (age, breed, and sex) may also aid in the formulation of a good diagnostic plan, as certain nervous system diseases may be more common in certain breeds or at certain ages. The initial findings may appear unrelated to nervous-system problems; however, it is not uncommon that nervous-system derangements are the most obvious clinical abnormalities in a larger, perhaps more diffuse disease process. In such cases, the signs of nervous-system derangement appear only as a clinical manifestation of that disease process in the nervous system. The general physical exam may well identify clinical manifestations of the larger disease process in other organ systems.

AT A GLANCE

- The neurological exam should always begin with a good history and general physical examination.

- The initial part of the nervous-system exam usually includes a cranial-nerve examination.

- The clinician's subjective interpretation of the horse's movement, body positions, and postures is an important part of the examination.

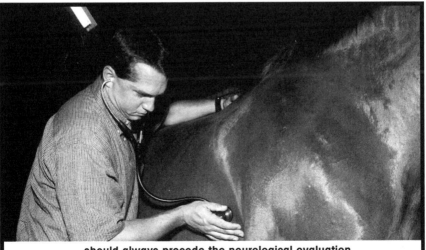

...should always precede the neurological evaluation.

A complete physical examination should be performed before initiating the more specific neurologic evaluation. Such an exam includes evaluation of all other organ systems (respiratory, gastrointestinal, integumentary, musculoskeletal, lymphatic, etc.). A rectal temperature should be obtained and routine blood work evaluation should be considered. Findings on a general physical examination may have significant implications on the interpretation of the neurologic examination findings. The general physical exam enables the clinician to interpret clinical findings with a more complete clinical picture of the abnormalities and their potential causes. For example, central nervous

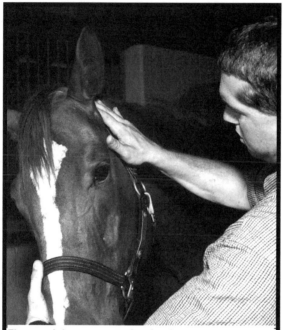

The cranial nerve examination is a key component of any complete nervous system examination.

system abnormalities may suggest more diffuse disease when found with rectal palpation of a mass in the abdomen. After the general physical exam is completed, the neurologic examination is initiated. The initial part of the nervous-system exam usually includes a cranial-nerve examination, which is a key component of any complete nervous-system examination. The clinician evaluates the functions of each of the 12 pairs of cranial nerves (nerves of the head that exit from the central-nervous-system areas of the brain and brainstem). Some cranial nerves cannot be evaluated thoroughly without the aid of electrical equipment or other assistance. For example, Cranial Nerve I (the olfactory nerve) is associated with the sense of smell — a sense that is difficult to evaluate in an animal incapable of spoken language.

REVIEW OF THE CRANIAL NERVES AND THEIR FUNCTIONS

Cranial Nerve I (olfactory nerve): sense of smell

Cranial Nerve II (optic nerve): vision

Cranial Nerve III (oculomotor nerve): movement of one of the muscles controlling eye movement and constriction of the pupil

Cranial Nerve IV (trochlear nerve): movement of one of the muscles controlling eye movement

Cranial Nerve V (trigeminal nerve): sensation of the face and head; movement of the muscles involved in chewing

Cranial Nerve VI (abducens nerve): movement of one of the muscles controlling eye movement

Cranial Nerve VII (facial nerve): movement of facial muscles; taste

Cranial Nerve VIII (vestibulocochlear nerve): hearing, sense of balance

Cranial Nerve IX (glossopharyngeal nerve): swallowing, gag reflex, taste, blood-pressure reflex

Cranial Nerve X (vagus nerve): swallowing; movement of voice box; control of many involuntary reflexes, including heart rate, gut motility, and blood-pressure reflex

Cranial Nerve XI (spinal-accessory nerve): movement of muscles high on the neck and shoulder

Cranial Nerve XII (hypoglossal nerve): tongue movement

Problems relating to the cranial nerves are manifested as abnormalities with the specific movements, reflexes, or sensations associated with that nerve.

A somatic reflex is an automatic response by a stimulated nerve, which triggers a muscle to produce a movement. The horse does not need to be conscious of the stimulation for the reflex to happen (think of your "knee-jerk" reflex). Some reflexes can be evaluated to a limited extent in the horse.

One, called the panniculus reflex, is the horse's skin-shake response to being touched along the trunk of the body. Another, called the "slap test," is frequently used to test for cervical spinal-cord lesions. In the slap test, the clinician evaluates the movement of the throat cartilage in response to a slap on the withers on the opposite side. The results of this test may increase the suspicion of a cervical spinal or brain-stem disorder but cannot itself be deemed diagnostic.

Some reflexes are controlled by the autonomic nervous system and also can be evaluated. An example of a reflex of this type is the pupil's constricting in bright light (the pupillary light reflex). Much of the unconscious information that is sent to the brain is information that stimulates reflexes. Such information is involved in reflexes that control gut motility, alertness, blood pressure, and many other vital functions.

Assessing a horse's movement is important.

A major component of an equine nervous-system evaluation is the clinician's subjective interpretation of the horse's movement, body positions, and postures. This part of the exam most often reveals information about the animal's ability to sense and control its own body parts in space. Problems related to deficits of this sensation lead to poorly coordinated movement called ataxia. The deficits that lead to ataxia are termed proprioceptive deficits, in reference to the receptors that relay information on body position. Many of the problems that produce proprioceptive deficits and ataxia occur in the spinal cord. However, ataxia may also be caused by dysfunction of higher centers of the nervous system, such as the cerebellum. For this reason, it is important that any nervous-system examination be complete so that other abnormalities in the examination that could indicate problems in areas of the nervous system other than the spinal cord can be considered and identified.

The typical limb-placement tests, such as the examiner manually crossing the limbs of the patient, require the horse to identify a malpositioned limb and to correct it. A better way to perform this test may be to place the limb in an abnormal position or location and to place force on the horse's body in order to compromise its stability. This may be preferable because some horses are highly cooperative and do not mind adopting unusual positions when asked to do so. Placing the force on the body forces the horse to sense the location of its limb and the instability of the position and to correct it.

Evaluation of strength, symmetry, and sizes of muscles is often used as an indirect evaluation of the motor nerve input to the muscle group(s) evaluated. Despite the fact that muscle weakness, atrophy (shrinkage), or asymmetry are commonly associated with central-nervous-system problems, such findings are not specific for motor nerve damage. Many other possible causes of muscle atrophy and weakness do exist. Other causes of muscle weakness and atrophy unrelated to the nervous system should be strongly considered if no signs of nervous-system impairment besides muscle weakness or atrophy exist. Severe atrophy can occur when the nerve supplying an affected muscle becomes severely impaired or nonfunctional, as in the case of a lesion that affects the origin of the nerve in the spinal cord (the central nervous system). Also, damage to the nerve as it courses its way to a muscle or other organ outside of the central nervous system (i.e., in the peripheral nervous system) can produce atrophy, weakness and/or asymmetry due to nerve damage. A clinician may be suspicious of nerve damage to a muscle or group of muscles if there are distinct nervous system sensory deficits that are clearly discerned relating to the same or another area of the nervous system. However, the most accurate way to characterize muscle weakness, atrophy, or asymmetry due to nerve damage is to test the nerve supplying the muscle electrically by electromyography, a technique that displays the nerve activity to the muscle.

REACHING A DIAGNOSIS

Generally speaking, the more complete the diagnostic evaluation, the more accurate the diagnosis is likely to be. This is especially true when the diagnosis involves the nervous system — in particular, in cases of mild or questionable abnormalities that are determined by a nervous-system evaluation. However, a diagnosis based solely on a neurologic examination is likely to be inaccurate. Any abnormalities detected during a complete examination (a nervous-system exam and a general physical) should be interpreted in light of all neurological and non-neurological disorders that could explain the findings. Common diagnostic procedures performed in association with the complete examination

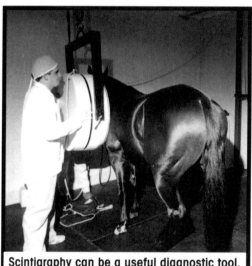

Scintigraphy can be a useful diagnostic tool.

include radiographs, blood work, spinal-fluid analysis, myelography, and nuclear scintigraphy.

Evaluation of a horse's response to treatment is frequently used to help support or refute a previously diagnosed condition. Although this is necessary for diagnostic evaluations that are restricted to the general physical and nervous-system examinations, such evaluation may lead to inaccurate conclusions because many nervous-system disorders are treated with similar medications and similar therapies. Any number or combination of such treatments could therefore prove helpful. Indeed, some of the treatments for nervous-system disorders are so broad that they may well improve conditions that mimic nervous-system disorders but that are not neurological in origin.

CHAPTER 3

Diseases that Affect the Peripheral and Central Nervous Systems

Numerous diseases can affect the horse's peripheral nervous system, and the accompanying clinical symptoms depend on which nerve or nerves are involved.

These nerves are, by definition, affected outside of the central nervous system and therefore may include any of the spinal nerves or the cranial nerves (I-XII) outside of the brain, the brainstem, and the spinal cord. Inflammation, infection, or physical impingement on a nerve can cause dysfunction in the nerve.

Because the nerve is affected outside of the central nervous system, the part of the body that shows a clinical abnormality is restricted to the area supplied by the affected nerve. Because the peripheral nerves are branches of the larger and more universally controlling central nervous system, the clinically abnormal area is smaller the further from the spinal cord that the nerve is affected. Furthermore, the closer a lesion is to the central nervous system — the more centralized the lesion's location — the larger the affected area. Therefore, a lesion that causes dysfunction of a nerve in a horse's lower leg will exhibit a smaller area of clinical abnormality — and fewer clinical signs — than one that causes dysfunction of a nerve located high on a leg, close to where it leaves the spinal column.

Diseases or conditions that affect the peripheral nervous system include:

Trauma/inflammation

Stringhalt

Post-anesthetic neuropathy

Neuropathy due to recumbency

Painful neuromas

Light-induced headshaking

Tumors

Infections/abscesses

Laryngeal hemiplegia ("roaring")

Otitis media/interna

Toxins

Neuromuscular disorders

Genetic disorders

The cause of a peripheral-nervous-system disorder may be specific to the peripheral nervous system, or it also may affect the central nervous system. Conditions such as trauma/inflammation, infections/abscesses, toxins, and tumors are more generalized and can affect both central and peripheral nervous systems; the other conditions listed above are associated more specifically with the peripheral nervous system. Of all the conditions, trauma is probably the most common cause of peripheral-nervous-system dysfunction.

DISEASES THAT AFFECT THE CENTRAL NERVOUS SYSTEM

The spinal cord carries the major nerve tracts to and from the brain. Tracts that descend from the brain and brainstem (motor tracts) are formed by aggregation of the fibers from various areas of the brain and brainstem and branch off the spinal cord at various levels to form the peripheral nerves. Tracts that ascend to the brain and brainstem (sensory tracts) are formed by aggregation of the fibers from the peripheral nerves en route to the brain and brainstem and also comprise part of the peripheral nerves. Because the motor and sensory fiber tracts supply diffuse areas of the body, disease of one or both tracts produces wide-ranging clinical signs, both internal and external.

Diseases that affect the highest centers — the brain and brainstem — can lead to far-reaching nervous-system abnormalities. If the brain is affected, then complex functions involving behavior and other high functions also may be affected. Diseases that affect the brain and brainstem also can cause abnormalities in the cranial nerves, which can lead to abnormal sensations or functions related to the special senses (taste, sight, hearing, balance, and smell) and to dysfunction of the motor and sensory functions of the nerves that supply the head and related regions.

The following diseases or conditions can affect the central nervous system:

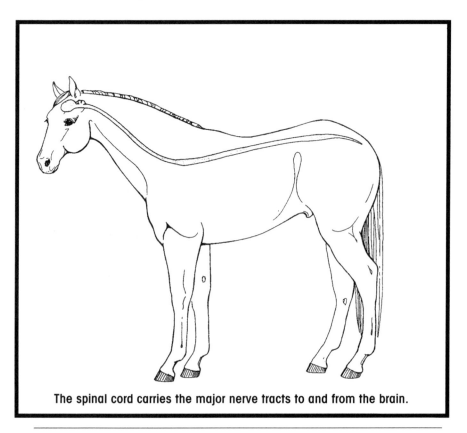

The spinal cord carries the major nerve tracts to and from the brain.

Trauma/inflammation

Equine protozoal myeloencephalitis (EPM)

Equine herpes virus I

Eastern/Western/Venezuelan equine encephalitis

Lyme disease

Streptococcus equi

Bacterial infection

Aberrant parasite migration

Rabies

Other viruses

Genetic disorders

Cervical compressive myelopathy ("wobbler syndrome")

Occipitoatlantoaxial malformation

Cerebellar abiotrophy

Narcolepsy

Epilepsy (idiopathic seizures)

Lysosomal storage diseases

Equine degenerative myelopathy (EDM)

Toxins

Tumors

Metabolic abnormalities

Polyneuritis equi (Cauda equina)

Equine motor neuron disease (EMND)

Lightning strike

CHAPTER 4

Infectious Nervous-System Disorders

Equine protozoal myeloencephalitis (EPM) is an infectious disease caused by protozoa that induce inflammation within the central nervous system. The symptoms of this disease are typically referable to the spinal cord; however, because the parasites have been found in the brain and in other areas of the central nervous system, EPM can produce symptoms related to any part of the central nervous system. The parasites that have been associated with EPM include *Sarcocystis neurona* and *Neospora species.*

The typical EPM case presentation includes ataxia and asymmetric weakness (one side of the body is weaker than the other). The disease's clinical signs often are not explicable by only one site of involvement. Therefore, the typical case also exhibits clinical signs of multifocal lesions. Cranial-nerve deficits may occur but are uncommon; dysfunction of an individual cranial nerve should be evaluated as a possible symptom of another, more likely disorder.

Many people associate muscle atrophy with EPM; but this symptom, too, should be interpreted carefully, as most cases of EPM do not exhibit clinically significant muscle atrophy. Other findings or complaints commonly associated with EPM include back pain, poor performance, and lameness. Although such complaints can be associated with EPM, they are more commonly caused by neurologically unrelated problems. The clinician should eliminate other, more common causes of such problems before diagnosing EPM. A horse with EPM displays true nervous-system deficits. This is important because a spinal-fluid analysis (immunoblot analysis) is not a good diagnostic tool when used on non-neurologic horses. In fact, its positive predictive value (the likelihood that a horse that tests positive truly has EPM) is very low if the test is used on a non-neurologic horse.

AT A GLANCE

• Equine protozoal myeloencephalitis is caused by parasites that attack the central nervous system.

• The neurological form of equine herpes virus type I can produce such symptoms as fever, ataxia, and partial limb paralysis.

• Alphaviruses such as EEE and WEE can affect the central nervous system.

After a complete examination of the horse, the clinician should formulate a diagnostic plan. This plan may be more complex if the horse displays only subtle or questionable central-nervous-system signs. Regardless of the severity of the case, the diagnostic plan should be formulated so that all possible explanations of the abnormalities and complaints are

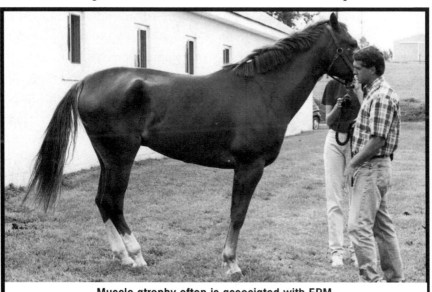

Muscle atrophy often is associated with EPM.

considered, one by one. If no diagnosis is reached during this elimination process, then a blood and cerebrospinal-fluid analysis for EPM are well warranted. In certain situations, such as in a recumbent animal or when ataxia is so severe as to endanger the clinician and co-workers, or when there is no access to personnel or equipment necessary for advanced diagnostics, it is impossible to rule out all possible causes of the problems. In such cases, it is not uncommon for a spinal-fluid analysis to be ordered earlier in the diagnostic process — a sometimes necessary but not ideal diagnostic decision, in terms of accuracy.

Equine spinal fluid can be collected from one of two locations. One site, called the cisterna magna, lies behind the skull and necessitates general anesthesia. The second site is the point of the lumbosacral space (location of a "hunter's bump"), on the midline of the back. Only sedation is required to collect fluid from the lumbosacral junction, but the location can prove a challenging one in terms of harvesting the fluid successfully and without blood contamination. Only experienced clinicians should perform this procedure.

The spinal fluid can be evaluated for blood contamination and antibody leakage into the cerebrospinal fluid (CSF). Using calculations called the albumin quotient and the IgG index may improve the accuracy of the interpretation of the results.

A spinal-fluid analysis is most useful in cases in which the analysis is negative on the immunoblot. EPM is considered highly unlikely in such cases, unless the onset of clinical signs was very recent. If symptoms did indeed begin recently, the spinal-fluid analysis should be repeated in a few weeks in case the antibody in the CSF had not yet been produced.

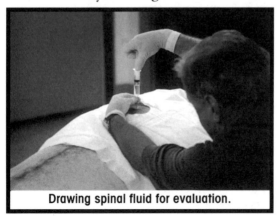

Drawing spinal fluid for evaluation.

What is more difficult is interpreting the positive EPM test. Researchers are learning that many horses that show no clinical signs of EPM may test positive in the CSF, for many possible reasons. In other words, a positive test by no means guarantees the presence and diagnosis of the disease. Furthermore, numerous studies have shown that positive blood samples indicate only exposure to the parasite, not clinical infection. Once again, a negative blood analysis may be useful because most such cases also have negative spinal-fluid test results. However, exceptions to this rule can occur, so a spinal-fluid analysis should never be used as a screening test for EPM. Instead, the spinal-fluid analysis should be used only in evaluating neurologically impaired horses.

To date, standard EPM therapy includes the administration of a drug called pyrimethamine at 1mg/kg/day, in combination with a sulfa antibiotic drug — usually sulfadiazine. Treatment is usually indicated for a minimum of 90 days. Unfortunately, there is no guarantee that treatment will lead to improvement — in large part because the diagnostic process for EPM is imperfect. Many treatment failures and perceived relapses occur simply because the original diagnosis was incorrect.

Relapses are not uncommon in cases of EPM — from five percent to nearly 30 percent, according to estimates. The duration of treatment and the type of medication used may affect relapse rates.

New treatments for EPM are on the horizon. Such drugs as toltrazuril (Baycox), diclazuril, and nitazoxanide may prove to be more effective than standard therapies. To date, only limited information is available on the use of these drugs, and no direct comparisons to standard treatment exist. Furthermore, the safety of these medications is poorly outlined.

Other treatments for EPM include oxytetracycline and acupuncture. Some advocates claim that such treatments can be effective, but their claims have not been scientifically evaluated in horses that have been rigorously evaluated for EPM. These claims of efficacy therefore could be very misleading.

Ancillary therapies for EPM are used in combination with the anti-protozoal treatment. Some practitioners prescribe the administration of folic acid to minimize the anemia associated with long-term treatment using standard therapy. However, the anemia related to EPM treatment seldom produces clinical signs, and horses absorb folic acid poorly; so folic-acid treatment cannot be recommended.

Vitamin E, steroids, butazolidin (Bute), Banamine, and other therapies may be helpful in controlling the inflammation associated with EPM. The use of these substances should be overseen by the treating veterinarian.

Response to therapy frequently is used to support or refute a diagnosis. Although this approach is necessary in cases of less-than-ideal diagnostic evaluations, it is likely to lead to erroneous conclusions because many treatments for EPM are non-specific; that is, they could potentially cause improvement in diseases and conditions other than EPM. In fact, even the antibiotic (sulfadiazine) that is used in combination with the pyrimethamine is broad in its spectrum of activity and therefore could cause improvement in other infectious conditions.

Many therapeutic regimens for EPM may include steroids, Bute, Banamine, homeopathic remedies, supplements, acupuncture, acupressure, massage therapy, and chiropractic therapy. Perhaps the most important treatment is rest. Indeed, thanks to the wide range of therapeutic combinations used and their broad-spectrum effects, any one such combination could produce improvement in other conditions, whether those conditions are neurologic or non-neurologic in origin. Therefore, clinical improvement is not proof positive of the presence of clinical EPM.

The prognosis for horses with EPM is variable and depends on the duration and severity of symptoms. Generally, horses that respond to treatment then plateau. Severely affected horses (those that are recumbent or severely debilitated) may respond enough to become pasture-sound and perhaps even breedable, but they are likely to have sustained permanent damage to the central nervous system. In the author's experience, many horses with moderate to severe residual nervous-system damage will be pasture-sound for a few years and eventually will succumb to the damage by falling and ultimately requiring euthanasia. Some severely affected horses may live much longer, but may represent the minority. Those less severely affected have recovered and returned to their previous use; some may actually improve in their performance.

EQUINE HERPES VIRUS I (EHV-I) ENCEPHALOMYELOPATHY

Equine herpes virus type I can cause several types of clinical disease in the horse. Perhaps the best known is the induction of abortion in pregnant mares. EHV-I is also capable of causing respiratory disease and a condition associated with the central nervous system. The neurological form of the disease, which is relatively uncommon, can be associated with abortion or respiratory infection. Unfortunately, EHV-I vaccine does not currently protect against the neurological form.

Horses contract EHV-I by inhaling the virus after infected horses have shed it in their nasal secretions. Typically, the pharyngeal (throat) lymph follicles and nodes pick up the virus, which then can spread by entering into certain cells of the immune system. The virus replicates in the walls of blood vessels when these immune cells enter the bloodstream. In the neurological form of the disease, the virus is associated with the blood vessels of the central nervous system, where it causes an immune-mediated vasculitis (inflammation of the blood vessels). This vasculitis leads to local inflammation of the central nervous system (hemorrhage and loss of blood supply), with obstruction of blood vessels and loss of local blood supply. Affected sites may include the brain and spinal cord.

The neurological form of EHV-I usually produces clinical signs a week to 10 days after infection. Symptoms may include fever, ataxia, partial limb paralysis, and loss of tone in the tail muscles and the anus, along with the dribbling of urine. Clinical abnormalities are often symmetric in appearance, and hind limbs are generally more affected than forelimbs. Affected stallions and geldings may exhibit penile flaccidity. Mares may have flaccidity of the vulva. Sensory deficits are much less common. Overall clinical presentation depends on the sites of the central nervous system affected.

The diagnosis of EHV-I encephalomyelopathy is suggested by the clinical findings and by the sudden onset of clinical signs. A history of fever, viral abortion, or respiratory disease also may be indicative of the disease, facilitating a tentative diagnosis. Further evaluation is helpful in reaching a more definitive diagnosis. Diagnostics can include four-fold increases in the serum antibody level of anti-EHV-I antibody in acute and convalescent serum samples (10 to 21 days apart), and spinal-fluid analysis. The spinal fluid from horses with EHV-I encephalomyelopathy is usually slightly yellow in appearance as a result of increased protein levels. Antibodies to EHV-I are not normally in the CSF; their presence is strongly suggestive of EHV-I encephalomyelopathy, provided that the spinal fluid is not contaminated with antibody-containing blood. As in the use of spinal-fluid analysis in diagnosing EPM, antibody leakage into the CSF is possible even when there is no CSF blood contamination. Blood contamination and antibody leakage can be evaluated by using the albumin quotient and the IgG index. Not all horses with EHV-I encephalomyelopathy have EHV-I antibodies in the CSF.

Treatment of EHV-I encephalomyelopathy is primarily supportive. Because the virus is contagious, isolation of the infected horses from other horses is necessary. Try to keep the animal standing, and minimize trauma and infections by providing good footing and administering prophylactic broad-spectrum antibiotics. Feed and water should be easily accessible, and the horse must be kept well hydrated. If it suffers from bladder dysfunction, an aseptically maintained urinary catheter is necessary. Use of a catheter also will minimize urine scalding. If scalding is present, one can wash the affected area regularly and apply a water-repellent ointment. If the horse becomes recumbent, more intensive management is needed to minimize muscle damage. Turn a recumbent horse over to the opposite side every two to four hours. It can be helped to stand with the assistance of a sling.

Treat inflammation of the central nervous system with the appropriate anti-inflammatory drugs, such as Bute, Banamine, and corticosteroids. Corticosteroids also can be helpful in treating the immune basis of the disease. Dimethylsulfoxide (DMSO) is commonly administered for its anti-inflammatory and free-radical-scavenging effects.

Horses that remain standing generally have a favorable prognosis. Generally, more severe deficits require a longer recovery period. Urinary control is frequently the first lost capacity to return, but some horses do remain incontinent. Recumbent animals, which are more likely to suffer from complications such as bladder infections, decubital ulcers, gastrointestinal problems, and muscle damage, have a less favorable prognosis. If complications begin to occur more frequently and to become more severe, the owner may need to consider euthanasia. Owners of severely affected horses should be aware that complete recovery from neurological EHV-I may take a year or more — and that some animals never completely recover as a result of permanent nervous-system damage.

VIRAL ENCEPHALITIS

Alphavirus Encephalitis (Eastern, Western, and Venezuelan Equine Encephalitis — EEE/WEE/VEE)

These viruses are characterized by their having "reservoirs" in wild animals (such as birds and small mammals), which themselves do not become clinically diseased. Certain insects — typically mosquitoes — are "vectors" that transmit the viral particles when they bite and ingest the infected blood of the wildlife reservoirs. The height of the vector season thus is the time period with the largest disease occurrence.

Clinical signs of disease are worse in unvaccinated animals.

Initial symptoms may include fever, anorexia, and stiffness; depression often follows. Many cases of WEE do not progress beyond these clinical signs, but EEE tends to continue to progress. After the onset of nervous-system signs, the blood-borne phase of the virus is usually over. Signs of brain impairment may occur next. The horse may pace restlessly or may show signs of depression, aggression, or hyperexcitability. Proprioceptive deficits may become apparent. As the disease progresses, further brain impairment may occur along with cranial-nerve dysfunction. Head-pressing, blindness, circling, head-tilting, muscle tremors, and seizures may ensue. Paralysis of the throat muscles and tongue are believed to be relatively common. Affected horses that become recumbent have a poor prognosis. Animals that survive require weeks to months for improvement.

The clinical presentation of VEE may be similar or somewhat different to those of EEE and WEE. In cases of VEE, diarrhea, depression, recumbency, and death may occur before neurologic deficits become evident.

A diagnosis of viral encephalitis is based on history, clinical findings, blood-antibody analysis, and post-mortem findings. A four-fold increase in antibodies in acute and convalescent titers is considered grounds for a positive diagnosis. Because such titer changes can be missed, using more than one type of antibody analysis can improve diagnostic accuracy. A more specific antibody test is available for confirming VEE.

Treatment for these diseases is primarily supportive and consists mainly of the same broad-spectrum measures used to control inflammation and edema in other nervous-system diseases: Bute, Banamine, and dimethylsulfoxide (DMSO). The use of corticosteroids is popular, but these substances should be used judiciously to prevent secondary bacterial infections. For this reason, antibiotic therapy may be warranted as well. Seizures must be controlled using diazepam (Valium), phenobarbital, and/or phenytoin. Adequate supportive care includes maintaining proper hydration and adequate caloric intake. If a horse is incapable of eating on its own, intravenous feeding may be necessary.

Complete recovery from these diseases is rare, and many animals are left with permanent nervous-system dysfunction. The mortality rate is reported to be 75 to 100 percent for EEE, 20 to 50 percent for WEE, and 40 to 80 percent for VEE.

Preventive measures include vaccination and the reduction of exposure to potential insect vectors. Annual EEE/WEE/VEE vaccinations should be administered in the late spring or a few months prior to exposure to insect vectors. Adequate antibody levels exist for between six and eight months. In regions with longer "bug seasons," horses should be vaccinated at least twice a year.

These viruses are transmissible from horses to humans in certain instances. Ordinarily, there is not enough virus in the blood of EEE-infected horses for the disease to be transmitted to humans. WEE cannot be transmitted to humans, but human WEE cases parallel the occurrence of equine cases and exposure to insect vectors. The VEE virus circulates at adequate blood levels for it to be transmitted to other animals and possibly to humans. Virus particles are plentiful in the nervous systems of affected animals, so precautions are necessary when performing necropsy examinations on suspect cases.

Flavivirus Encephalitis

Like the alphaviruses, these viruses are transmitted to horses by insects such as mosquitoes and ticks. Birds are common wildlife hosts, and subclinical infections can occur in other livestock. In general, clinical infection is sporadic and infrequent, but these viruses are capable of causing disease in humans. Japanese B encephalitis is more common in humans, and humans are often the source of animal infection. Borna disease and near-Eastern equine encephalomyelitis occur as accidental infections in the horse. Symptoms of these diseases are similar to other equine encephalidities, but may vary more widely for Japanese B encephalitis.

Treatment is similar to that of other viral encephalidities. Effective vaccinations are available, but are generally not administered in this country due to the diseases' infrequent occurrence.

RABIES

Although they are not the most commonly affected animals (skunks, raccoons, and foxes are affected most frequently), horses can and do contract rabies. This disease, for which there is no cure, is a significant health hazard to humans and domestic animals as well as to horses, and people can contract rabies from horses.

A horse can contract rabies if it is bitten by an infected animal (the most common mode of transmission), inhales virus-laden particles, or swallows virus-laden saliva. A pregnant mare can transmit rabies to her unborn foal via the placenta.

Rabies virus spreads from the site of contamination to the central nervous system by moving through the peripheral nerves — a process that can take days to several weeks, depending on how close the bite site is to the central nervous system. After it invades the central nervous system, it can replicate and spread rapidly.

Clinical signs of rabies are highly variable and range from obscure lameness and colic to sudden death without other signs. Other clinical signs seen in horses may include aggressive behavior changes, muscle tremors, seizures, depression, anorexia, head tilt, circling, excessive salivation, facial and pharyngeal (throat) paralysis, blindness, inability to urinate normally, self-mutilation, and generalized paralysis. Clinical signs progress rapidly in most affected horses, and death occurs within five to 10 days.

It is difficult to make a definitive diagnosis of rabies before death. Other nervous-system diseases should be considered in suspicious cases; but if rabies is considered a possible cause, specific precautions and isolation are essential to minimize exposure to humans and other animals. All biologic samples harvested from a rabies suspect must be handled specially. If the animal dies or is euthanized, the case must be reported to the authorities, the animal's head must be submitted according to law, and the brain must be tested for specific microscopic lesions caused by the rabies virus. All human exposures must be well documented. If the brain tests positive for rabies, all humans and other animals that were exposed to the infected horse must receive antibody vaccinations.

The best protection against rabies is regular vaccination of all animals. The vaccine is relatively inexpensive and should be considered part of any complete vaccination program. The initial series of the vaccine includes two or three boosters administered at two- to four-week intervals; initial vaccination of a single dose without follow-up boosters may be less likely to confer adequate immunity. Unvaccinated horses that are exposed to rabies must be quarantined for several months and euthanized if they begin to exhibit the telltale symptoms of the disease.

OTITIS MEDIA/INTERNA (OM/I)

OM/I is an infectious and inflammatory condition that affects the middle and inner ear. This process is usually restricted to just outside of the central nervous system, where two of the twelve cranial nerves lie close to the middle-ear cavity. The two nerves typically involved are cranial nerve VII (the facial nerve) and cranial nerve VIII (the vestibulocochlear nerve). In severe cases, the condition can spread to the central nervous system.

Equine OM/I has only recently received attention and may go undiagnosed or misdiagnosed for much or all of the disease course. The disease may be underdiagnosed in horses because many of the clinical signs seen are often attributed to EPM. The origins of OM/I are still unclear; it may be associated with upper-respiratory infections (viral or bacterial) or with the anatomy and function of the equine ear canal.

Clinical signs of OM/I involve dysfunction of the affected

A horse with OM/I.

cranial nerves: facial-nerve paralysis, deviation of the muzzle away from the affected side, and drooping of the eyelid and ear on the affected side. Vestibulocochlear-nerve deficits may manifest as ataxia that worsens when the horse is blindfolded, abnormal body posture, leaning against walls toward the side of the lesion, circling in the direction of the affected side, tilting the head toward the side of the lesion, nystagmus (oscillating horizontal movement of the pupils), and hearing loss. Recumbent horses lie on the side of the lesion. Some symptoms may vary if the lesion involves the cerebellum's input for balance and coordination. Drainage from the affected ear may be seen. In rare cases, horses exhibit the disease in both ears.

Diagnosing OM/I involves identifying the clinical signs of cranial-nerve deficits. Evaluation for other evidence of central-nervous-system problems can help rule out CNS disease. Diagnostic evaluation typically includes skull radiographs and guttural-pouch endoscopy. Cases of extended duration may exhibit changes in the stylohyoid bone and the tympanic bulla. Skull X-rays can be difficult to interpret, especially earlier in the disease process. Endoscopic examination of the guttural pouch on the affected side may also reveal bony changes associated with the stylohyoid bone and with its joint with the temporal bone of the skull. In instances in which X-rays and endoscopic examination reveal no changes, bone-phase nuclear scintigraphy may identify the active lesion.

Treatment of OM/I involves broad-spectrum antimicrobials, or more specific antimicrobial coverage if middle-ear fluid is obtained for culture under general anesthesia. Anti-inflammatory medications can help control or reduce the accumulation of fluid and the inflammation of the middle and inner ear. If central-nervous-system involvement is suspected, more aggressive antimicrobial and anti-inflammatory therapies are warranted. Most horses recover. Some of the more severe cases may have long-term nervous-system deficits.

BACTERIAL AND FUNGAL MENINGITIS

Bacterial and fungal meningitis are infections that involve the tissue layers over the brain and spinal cord that contain the cerebrospinal fluid. The presence of bacteria or fungi in the spinal fluid causes irritation of these tissue layers and leads to the development of clinical signs associated with the resulting inflammation and edema. In rare cases, meningitis can be caused by fungi and also can involve the brain tissue, leading to encephalitis.

Bacterial or fungal meningitis is not typically encountered in horses with healthy immune systems. It can be associated with poor colostrum intake in neonatal or pediatric foals and can lead to septicemia (bacteria-infected blood) that seeds the central nervous system. Other infectious processes may cause abscessation of related areas of the brain or spinal cord such as a vertebral body or brain abscess. Such abscesses that break open then seed the central nervous system with bacteria. These abscesses can be associated with rare cases of strangles (*streptococcus equi*). Bacterial meningitis may occur as an extension of an infectious process from the inner ear (OM/I). Other possible causes include trauma and sinus infection. Such scenarios are most likely when fractures of the temporal bone occur in association with OM/I, allowing bacteria in the middle and inner ear to enter into the cerebrospinal fluid.

Clinical signs of meningitis include fever, depression, stiff neck and neck pain, ataxia with spasticity, "stargazing," abnormal vocalization, and seizures. Diagnosis consists of identifying the clinical signs, determining a compatible history, and examining the cerebrospinal fluid (CSF). CSF cell analysis shows increased numbers of inflammatory cells that may harbor bacteria. A positive CSF culture or the identification of bacteria on a sample of CSF obtained via sterile procedure confirms the diagnosis of bacterial meningitis.

Treatment of bacterial meningitis involves the administration of potent antimicrobial drugs that effectively penetrate into the central nervous system from the blood. Frequently, intensive supportive care is necessary. Anti-inflammatory drugs are frequently used to control the inflammation and edema associated with the condition. Corticosteroids are generally not advisable, as they may make the infection worse. However, as with any CNS disorder, their use may become necessary to control severe inflammation. Seizures are not uncommon and must be controlled with anti-seizure drugs such as diazepam, phenobarbital, and phenytoin.

The prognosis for horses with bacterial meningitis is guarded; the prognosis for horses with fungal meningitis is worse. Severe infections often lead to death or require euthanasia. Seizures may become uncontrollable, even with high doses of anti-seizure medications. Early detection, along with appropriate antimicrobials and intensive care, may produce better outcomes.

PARASITIC ENCEPHALOMYELOPATHY

Various types of migrating parasites may find their way to the equine central nervous system in infrequent instances, causing damage and clinical signs of derangement. Clinical signs usually exhibit rapid onset, are asymmetrical, and depend on the site(s) affected. Either the spinal cord or the brain can be affected. Migrating helminth worms or fly larvae are the most common types of parasites. Species include *strongylus, draschia, hypoderma,* and *habronema* flies; *setaria;* and *halicephalobus.*

Diagnosis consists of identifying an increase in eosinophils or neutrophils (types of inflammatory cells) in the cerebrospinal fluid — a finding that may not be present in all cases.

If appropriate antiparasitic treatments are administered

promptly, treatment can be effective. Typical antiparasitic agents used are ivermectin, fenbendazole, thiabendazole, and diethylcarbamazine. Most of these medications (except diethylcarbamazine) are the active ingredients in many commonly administered paste dewormers. Anti-inflammatory therapy may be necessary to control the central-nervous-system inflammation associated with the parasites and their death in the CNS. Medications such as Bute, Banamine, and corticosteroids should be considered.

Prognosis for this disorder depends on the rapidity of diagnosis and treatment. As the disease progresses and clinical signs worsen, the prognosis follows. As in any CNS disease that leads to recumbency, the prognosis becomes poor.

LYME-DISEASE-RELATED NEUROLOGICAL DISORDERS

Lyme disease is caused by the organism *Borrelia burgdorferi* and is reported to occur in horses to a limited extent. Most of the disease's clinical signs in horses relate to shifting leg lameness as a result of arthritis in the affected joints. However, there have been reports of nervous-system disorders (neuroborreliosis) in humans with Lyme disease. At least one report exists that associates Lyme disease with CNS signs and lesions at post-mortem in a horse. The affected horse exhibited propulsive walking, head-tilting, throat and tail paralysis, and aimless wandering. The report could not exclude other possible causes of encephalitis but concluded that the findings were strongly suggestive of neuroborreliosis.

As there has been only one unconfirmed report of neuroborreliosis in horses, the risk to any individual horse is likely to be small. Still, the treatment of choice is prevention. Minimize horses' exposure to ticks, particularly those in at-risk areas. Remove all ticks from horses promptly. If a horse is diagnosed with Lyme disease, prompt treatment using appropriate antimicrobials — such as tetracycline, erythromycin, high doses of penicillin, and third-generation cephalosporins (Naxcel) — is necessary.

CHAPTER 5

Trauma-Induced Neurological Disorders; Inflammatory Conditions

Trauma is one of the most common causes of nervous-system dysfunction, both of the central and the peripheral nervous systems. Trauma typically causes either inflammation of or direct physical damage to a nerve, thereby impeding its function. Dysfunction caused by inflammation is more responsive to treatment than that caused by physical damage, such as the partial or complete severing of a nerve.

In the peripheral nervous system, the site of the trauma dictates the associated symptoms. Depending on the severity of the damage or inflammation, complete or incomplete loss of nerve function may result. The closer that the damage site is to the nerve's origin from the spinal cord, the larger the affected area.

Trauma to unrelated tissue, such as bone or surrounding soft tissue,

Trauma can cause nervous-system dysfunction.

occasionally may cause inflammation and dysfunction of nearby nerves. In other cases, the main damage may be only to the nerves themselves, as in a case of severe stretching or tearing of the nerves that supply a limb at the very site of their exit from the spinal cord. In such an area of the forelimb, the nerves are all interconnected as they emerge from the spinal cord, forming a network called a plexus. The plexus in the forelimb is called the brachial plexus

> ## AT A GLANCE
>
> • Trauma is a common cause of nervous-system dysfunction.
>
> • Trauma can cause loss of nerve function, depending on the severity.
>
> • Trauma to the spinal column frequently leads to signs of nervous-system dysfunction, such as ataxia, loss of sensation, and weakness.

and can sustain damage when a horse falls. The injury affects the entire forelimb, and the horse will be unable to bear weight or to extend the limb; there also may be pain and swelling in the area between the forearm and the chest. Recovery is possible but depends on the severity of the damage. A complete tearing of these nerves (avulsion) from their origin carries a poor prognosis. A horse that recovers from a brachial-plexus injury may have long-term limb problems that end its competitive career.

Another peripheral nerve that is susceptible to trauma is the suprascapular nerve, which serves the upper muscles of the shoulder. Damage to this nerve may lead to severe atrophy of the muscle above the spine of the scapula, a condition often referred to as Sweeney.

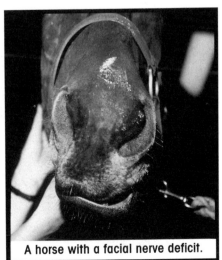

A horse with a facial nerve deficit.

Trauma to a cranial nerve that occurs outside of the central nervous system results in signs of dysfunction associated with the specific functions of that nerve. Some cranial nerves, such as facial nerve VII, have quite a long course outside of the central nervous system, which makes this nerve also fairly susceptible to trauma and inflammation. Therefore, a cranial-nerve deficit does not necessarily indicate that the horse has a central-nervous-system problem. If only one nerve, such as the facial nerve, which has a long course outside of the central nervous system, is affected, the cause is more likely to be peripheral-nervous-system dysfunction.

Trauma to the central nervous system tends to be more serious in nature. The clinical signs may be more striking and involve larger portions of the body as a result of the damage to the ascending and descending spinal-cord nerve tracts or to higher centers of the central nervous system involved in controlling many bodily functions.

Trauma to the spinal column frequently leads to signs of nervous-system dysfunction, such as ataxia, loss of sensation in affected regions, and weakness. This dysfunction may occur as a result of direct physical damage to the spinal cord or of trauma-induced inflammation. As there is little room in the spinal canal to allow for swelling of the spinal cord, any inflammation may lead to compression of the cord in that region. Between the compression and the inflam-

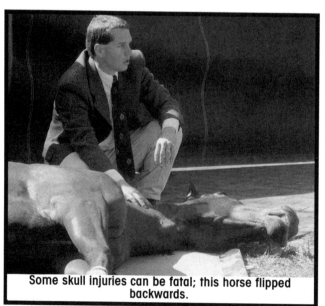
Some skull injuries can be fatal; this horse flipped backwards.

matory process, dysfunction of the nerve tracts in the affected areas of the cord is likely. But as the swelling and inflammation are resolved, the nerve tracts may resume their full
function.

Vertebral fractures or luxation (partial dislocation) of the
joints of the spinal column also can cause compression, which
itself can lead to inflammation and swelling that exacerbate
the compression. Some vertebral fractures even can partially or
completely sever the spinal cord. If the cord is completely
severed, the horse will be unable to stand due to weakness and
will be unable to consciously move any part of his body below
the injury site. Limb reflexes are still present, but they become
exaggerated, and the horse is unable to perceive the stimulus.
Most important, the segmental reflexes do not disappear with
cord transection, except at the level of the transection.

Common sites of spinal-cord injury are the joint of the first
bone of the spinal column with the skull, the lower neck,
and the middle back. Skull injuries or blows to the poll —
even if they do not result in fracture — may affect the bone
compartment of the brain (calavarium) and the basisphenoid bone. Basisphenoid or other fractures may cause severe
hemorrhaging and/or edema, which may cause the brainstem to herniate through the bone hole that surrounds the
junction of the upper spinal cord with the brainstem. Such
injuries and herniation are severe and frequently are fatal. If
a horse is able to recover from a basisphenoid-bone fracture
or poll trauma, it may still lose its sight as a result of stretching or avulsion of the optic nerve.

Injuries to the brainstem can be even more serious and life-
threatening than spinal-cord injuries because the medulla
contains centers that govern breathing, consciousness, heart
rate, and blood pressure. The 12 pairs of cranial nerves generally exit from the spinal cord at the levels of the medulla and
the brainstem. As a result, conditions that affect these areas
may also produce dysfunction of the related nerves. Because
the control centers for the cranial nerves are close to one

another in the brainstem, a central-nervous-system problem may affect more than one cranial nerve and cause associated clinical signs. A severe injury to the brainstem and medulla is capable of causing instant death.

Damage to the cerebellum can produce a severe loss of co-ordinated movement (ataxia). Spinal-cord damage can produce ataxia as well, so it also must be considered as a possible cause when symptoms are present. However, cerebellar injuries are less common than spinal-cord injuries. Cerebellar injuries also may be accompanied by tremors, generalized weakness, nystagmus (rhythmic, involuntary eye movements), inaccurate timing of movements and coordination of muscle activity, abnormal body posture, and loss of equilibrium.

Injuries to the cerebrum can have wide-ranging clinical effects, from behavioral and sensory changes to loss of motor control and sensory function of the limbs. Because the cerebrum has such wide-ranging function and interconnections, the injury's location and severity dictates the clinical signs.

Treatment of traumatic and inflammatory injury of the nervous system is nonspecific. Most therapies aim to minimize edema, hemorrhage, and oxygen-derived free radicals by treating the injury and controlling inflammation. For more on these therapies, see the section on nonspecific therapies in Chapter 12, "Management of the Neurologically Impaired Horse."

INFLAMMATORY CONDITIONS OF THE NERVOUS SYSTEM

Cranial Nerve Deficits Associated with Guttural-Pouch Infections/Inflammation

The guttural pouch is a large space that extends from the Eustachian tube (the ear tube). As it does in humans, the tube courses from the back of the throat to the middle ear. A few key cranial nerves run through the guttural pouch: IX, X, XI, and XII. A structure called the cranial cervical ganglion, which is associated with the sympathetic nervous system, also exits through the guttural pouch.

Clinical signs relating to dysfunction of these nerves can occur as a result of bacterial or fungal infection, inflammation, or other conditions of the guttural pouch. Symptoms may include Horner's syndrome (later in this chapter) and an inability to swallow normally (dysphagia).

Treatment of a guttural-pouch problem consists of resolving the cause of the inflammation, infection, or other irritation and may include anti-inflammatory therapy and frequent flushing of the affected side of the guttural pouch. On occasion, surgical intervention may be necessary. Quick and effective treatment usually results in complete recovery of cranial-nerve function. More severe and prolonged diseases and nerve deficits may result in incomplete recovery of nerve function.

Rupture of the Rectis Capitis Ventralis Muscle

The rectis capitis can rupture when a horse falls over backward and hyperextends its neck and head. Tearing of the tendon insertion of the muscle damages cranial nerves IX through XI. Clinical signs include bleeding from the nose, laryngeal hemiplegia, and an inability to swallow normally. Head and neck radiographs can confirm the diagnosis. Pre-existing guttural pouch infections can weaken the bone, predisposing a horse to injury. The neurologic abnormalities are treated symptomatically and with supportive care.

Laryngeal Hemiplegia

If the left side of a horse's neck sustains trauma or becomes inflamed — say, as a result of inappropriate administration of medication in the left jugular vein — the left recurrent laryngeal nerve may become paralyzed. This long nerve causes movement of the upper-airway cartilage (the left arytenoid cartilage); nerve dysfunction leads to an inability to retract the cartilage from the airway during exercise — a condition

Racehorses can suffer from airway obstruction, for which surgery often provides relief.

known as "roaring" due to the sound produced. The nerve does not exhibit the same course on the other side of the neck, and so right-sided paralysis of the arytenoid due to trauma or inflammation on the right side of the neck is uncommon.

Most horses do not perform at a level strenuous enough to be affected by the paralysis, and so most cases of roaring are left untreated. In severe cases, or in the case of a horse that exercises at maximal levels (such as a racehorse), the airway obstruction may be significant enough to impede performance. In such cases, the arytenoid can be surgically tied to an open position (a procedure known as a tie-back). Complications may include failure of the tie-back and recurrent aspiration of feed, which can lead to pneumonia.

Horner's Syndrome

Horner's syndrome is defined as the presence of a drooping eyelid, pupillary constriction, the appearance of an "inward setting" of the eyeball, protrusion of the third eyelid with possible blood-vessel dilation on the same side of the head, and increased facial temperature and sweating on the same side. Damage to a major sympathetic nerve trunk that passes near the jugular vein is often the cause of Horner's syndrome; it may also occur as part of a larger nervous-system problem or as a result of localized trauma. It has also been documented in association with uncomplicated intravenous injections.

Treatment for Horner's syndrome involves correcting the

cause of the damage or irritation to the affected nerve trunk and often involves anti-inflammatory drugs such as corticosteroids, Bute, and Banamine. Antimicrobials may be necessary to treat infectious conditions. Other medications may be directed at the treatment of other nervous-system diseases.

CHAPTER 6
Nervous-System Disorders Caused by Toxin

There are no specific antidotes to many of the toxins that cause nervous-system abnormalities. Diagnosis of these conditions may be strongly supported by the identification of the toxin or the toxin source in the stomach contents. Treatment consists largely of supportive care and the administration of medications or substances to prevent further toxin absorption from the gastrointestinal tract.

Some major causes of poisoning and their therapies are described below. In general, the more toxin a horse ingests, the more difficult the treatment is likely to be and the poorer the prognosis.

LEUKOENCEPHALOMALACIA (MOLDY-CORN POISONING)

Late fall to early spring is the prime period for this disease, which occurs as a result of a horse's ingesting corn infected with a fungus called *Fusarium moniliforme*, which produces a toxin called fumonisin B1. The disease can also occur in horses that consume commercially prepared diets. The infected corn kernels are pink to reddish-brown in color, and damaged kernels are more dangerous than undamaged kernels.

Two nervous-system syndromes may be associated with the ingestion of this toxin. The first involves liver damage and the associated hepatoencephalopathy (see Chapter 9, Disorders

Related to Metabolism and Organ Function). The second occurs as a direct result of the toxin's effects on the white matter of the cerebrum, the brainstem, the cerebellum, and/or the spinal cord. The result is death (necrosis) of these areas.

Clinical signs of moldy-corn poisoning include loss of coordination, propulsive walking, head-pressing, lethargy, blindness, hyperexcitability, profuse sweating, and delirium. Recumbency and convulsions precede death. Recovery is possible, but long-term nervous-system deficits are common.

Diagnosis is based primarily on clinical signs and on a history of exposure to moldy corn. Feed analysis may identify the toxin within a suspected feed source. Clinical abnormalities usually indicate concomitant evidence of liver damage. CSF analysis reveals increases in protein and cell counts out of reference range. Myelin basic protein concentrations may also be elevated.

There is no specific treatment for this disease; nor does a neutralizing antidote against the toxin exist. Treatment is essentially supportive and includes measures to combat the nervous-system and liver dysfunction. Nutritional support frequently is required, as are medications to control CNS swelling (edema). Heavy sedation to prevent self-inflicted trauma often is necessary. Activated charcoal can be administered by nasogastric tube to bind toxin not yet absorbed from the digestive tract if the intoxication is recent. Prevention involves ensuring that the feed is uncontaminated and that it is stored in conditions that inhibit mold growth. The overall prognosis may depend on a number of factors but is guarded at best. In some cases, euthanasia may be necessary.

OTHER CAUSES OF NERVOUS-SYSTEM DISORDERS

Toxic Plants and Fungi that Produce CNS Stimulation

Locoweed: *Astragalus* and *Oxytropis* species found in western Canada, the western United States, and northern Mexico.

Feed analysis may identify a toxin within a suspected feed source.

Nervous ergotism: a toxin produced by a number of alkaloids contained in a fungus found in some grains (wheat, barley, rye, and oats) and wild grasses called *Claviceps purpura*. Mostly a concern in wet climates or during wet periods.

Perennial ryegrass: production of neurotoxic alkaloids by a fungus that can grow on perennial ryegrass.

Toxic Plants and Fungi that Produce CNS Depression

Yellow star thistle, Russian knapweed: found in the western United States in nonirrigated pasture in the dry season. Continuous exposure and ingestion is probably needed to cause signs of intoxication.

White snakeroot, rayless goldenrod: White snakeroot is primarily found in the eastern half of the United States. Toxin exposure is greatest in dry years or in areas of inadequate pasture. Continuous exposure and ingestion or massive one-time ingestion are probably necessary to produce signs of intoxication. Rayless goldenrod is found in the southwestern United States and produces similar clinical signs of intoxication.

Black locust: intoxication in the horse is probably rare. Toxin is present in seeds, sap, roots, wood, leaves, and bark.

Bracken fern: found in forested areas or abandoned fields in the northern and western United States. Toxicity can occur year-round, but ingestion of this plant may be more common in times and areas of poor forage availability. Generally unpalatable to horses, but a taste for it may be developed. The entire plant is considered to be toxic.

Equisetum: commonly known as horsetail, mare's tail, or scouring rush. Unpalatable to horses. Intoxication most commonly associated with contaminated hay.

Milkweed: *Ascelapias* species. Generally unpalatable to horses. May contaminate hay.

Milkvetch: miser species of *Astragalus*. Found primarily in the western United States. Primarily toxic to ruminants, but reported to be poisonous to horses.

Sorghum: ataxia and urinary incontinence frequently is associated with the feeding of sorghum species. No specific diagnostic test exists. Treatment is supportive and symptomatic. Removal of the source of sorghum from the diet results in improvement of clinical signs.

Trichothecenes: compounds produced by fungi of the *Fusarium* species. Only a very few of these compounds are believed to be found naturally in feedstuffs, and only one of those has been associated with an intoxication.

Aflatoxins: toxins produced by fungi of the *Aspergillus flavus* and *Aspergillus parasiticus*. These fungi are found commonly in nature and are common in stored feeds. Under conditions of adequate temperature and humidity, these molds produce large amounts of aflatoxin. Most commonly affected are cereal grains, cottonseed meal, and peanuts. These toxins probably induce liver damage more than direct nervous-system damage. This disorder has been only infrequently documented.

Medicinal and Other Intoxications

Carbamates: found in pesticides. Readily absorbed through the lungs, gastrointestinal tract, and skin. Signs of intoxication relate to overstimulation of the parasympathetic division of the autonomic nervous system and include salivation, hypermotility of the gut, colic, diarrhea, tearing, pupillary constriction, urinary and fecal incontinence, muscle twitching, and stiffness. Diagnosis is made through history of exposure, clinical signs, and response to atropine treatment (the antiparasympathetic effect). Treatment involves administering atropine and may require repeat doses. Supportive care is also necessary.

Organophosphates: found in animal and plant insecticides, parasiticides, fungicides, herbicides, rodenticides, insect repellents, and sterilization solutions. Toxicity of these compounds is lessened through degradation by sun, water, microbes, alkali, or metal ions. Increased toxicity may occur as a result of storage activation or heat. Clinical signs are very similar to that of carbamate toxicity by overstimulation of the parasympathetic division of the autonomic nervous system. Diagnosis is made by history of exposure to these toxins and clinical signs. Treatment involves administering atropine; doses may need to be repeated. Additional treatment could include administration of 2-PAM (Pralidoxime Chloride), which has an additional direct effect of inactivating the effects of the toxins. The use of 2-PAM in horses may be prohibitively expensive in many instances. Supportive care is necessary.

Chlorinated hydrocarbons: found in older pesticides, insecticides, and parasiticides. Toxicity may occur with repeated exposure (the accumulation effect) or as a result of a single excessive exposure. Acts as a diffuse CNS depressant; symptoms may include seizures and muscular tremors, ataxia, salivation, dilated pupils, diarrhea, urination, and rapid heart rate. Diagnosis is made by history of exposure, clinical signs, and tissue concentrations. There is no antidote to these compounds. Supportive care, control of convulsions and hyperactivity with chloral hydrate or pentobarbital, and administration of activated charcoal to prevent further absorption should be considered in the treatment plan.

Strychnine: primarily used as a rodenticide. Intoxication in horses is rare. Clinical signs appear in as little as 10 minutes after ingestion and include apprehension and muscle stiffness, followed by seizures and possibly sweating and loss of coordination. Diagnosis is made by history of exposure, clinical signs, and rapid recovery in horses treated in time to prevent further complications. No specific antidote exists, and treatment is symptomatic and supportive. Sedation (usually using chloral hydrate or pentobarbital) frequently is required.

Metaldehyde: usually used to kill slugs and snails. Horses are poisoned by exposure to snail and slug bait. Clinical signs begin within one hour after ingestion and include profuse sweating, salivation, restlessness, loss of coordination, muscle spasms, and deep respiration. Diagnosis is made by history of exposure and clinical signs. No specific antidote exists. Treatment is symptomatic and supportive. Sedation and muscle relaxants may be useful.

Methiocarb: also used to kill snails and slugs. Clinical signs include severe muscle tremors, profuse sweating and salivation, colic, and increase in heart and respiratory rates. Specific antidote is atropine and often requires repeated dosing. Supportive care is also necessary.

4-Aminopyridine: used as a bird repellent and often mixed with grain. Clinical signs include profuse sweating, convulsions, behavior changes, and fluttering of the third eyelid. Diagnosis is made by history of exposure and clinical signs. No specific antidote exists. Supportive care is necessary.

Levamisole: used mostly as a dewormer in non-equine farm animals. Clinical signs occur within about one hour of administration and include hyperexcitability, muscle tremors, excessive salivation, and tearing. Horses may become recumbent but generally recover in 10 to 12 hours. Adverse effects are more common when administered as an injection. Diagnosis is made by history of administration and clinical signs. Treatment is supportive.

Carbon disulfide: formerly used as a common antiparasitic agent; now used as a solvent for resins, pesticides, and waxes and as an agent to control insects in stored grain. Clinical signs in acute cases include breathing difficulties, spastic tremors, convulsions, coma, and death. Chronic exposure may lead to behavior changes, peripheral nerve deficits, and dysfunction of the cranial nerves but is unlikely in horses.

Diagnosis is based on exposure and clinical signs. Treatment is symptomatic and supportive.

Nicotine: contained in tobacco leaves. Concentrated solutions of nicotine have been used to control leaf-eating insects. Clinical signs begin quickly and involve overstimulation of the parasympathetic nervous system, including excitement, salivation, and diarrhea; and are followed by ataxia, depression, slow respiration, and increased heart rate. Convulsions also may occur. Treatment is generally ineffective because of the rapid course of the toxicosis. Symptomatic treatments are administered along with measures to lessen the absorption of the toxin from the intestinal tract or through the skin.

Ammonia: toxicity occurs by primary exposure to ammonia gas or by urea toxicity within the body from body metabolism. Exposure to toxic levels of ammonia gas is rare. Clinical signs include irritation of the eyes and respiratory tract. At high levels, loss of eyesight and skin burns may occur. Diagnosis is based on history and clinical signs. Treatment involves removal from the source of exposure and symptomatic treatment.

Urea, nonprotein nitrogen: urea and nonprotein nitrogen are added to ruminant feed as a source of nitrogen for protein requirements. Urea is also used as fertilizer. Horses are mildly susceptible to urea toxicosis, and ingestion of urea-containing feedstuffs in sufficient quantities to cause clinical signs is unlikely. Horses are more susceptible to toxicity due to ammonium-salt ingestion, which can be lethal. Clinical signs begin rapidly and can include colic, weakness, breathing difficulties, convulsions, and rapid death. Progression may occur to include behavioral abnormalities, tremors, muscle twitching, and salivation. Diagnosis of urea, ammonia, and other nonprotein-nitrogen toxicity relies on history of exposure and clinical signs. Laboratory evaluation of blood-ammonia levels is possible, but results can be difficult to interpret. Treatment is symptomatic and usually ineffective.

Convulsing horses should be sedated using pentobarbital or other appropriate medications.

Atropine: overdose can produce colic, gastrointestinal stasis, and pupillary dilation.

Reserpine: used as a long-term tranquilizer and to stimulate lactation. Overdose may cause depression, colic, profuse sweating, increased gastrointestinal sounds, diarrhea, muscle trembling, pupillary constriction, prolapse of the penis in males, and flatulence. No specific antidote exists, but methamphetamine has been recommended.

Piperazine: widely used as a dewormer, especially in young horses. Toxicity is rare. Clinical signs are depression and loss of coordination. Diagnosis is based on history of treatment and clinical signs. The drug can be identified through urinalysis. No treatment other than supportive care is indicated. Complete recovery generally occurs in two to three days.

Phenothiazine tranquilizers: used as tranquilizers. Acepromazine and fluphenazine are two of the most commonly used. In rare cases, acepromazine may cause persistent protrusion of the penis in stallions. Treatment includes supportive care and relief of penile edema. Some stallions may fail to recover completely. If administered early in the clinical course, benztropine mesylate has been advocated as a treatment. Fluphenazine (Prolixin) is used as a long-term tranquilizer in horses. It is rarely associated with CNS signs of pawing, ataxia, hyperexcitability, muscle tremors, profuse sweating, intermittent depression, facial grimacing, recumbency, and seizures. Treatment may include the administration of diphenhydramine and pentobarbital as well as supportive care.

Procaine: commonly found in intramuscular formulations of Penicillin G. Clinical signs include rapid respiration, agitation, pacing, muscle tremors, propulsive walking, ataxia, falling, and recumbency. Toxic reactions are probably more common when procaine penicillin is administered partially into a blood vessel. Treatment involves sedation when possible. Most toxic episodes last no more than 20 to 30 minutes, but the animal may appear to be depressed afterward.

Propylene glycol: used to dilute many injectable medications. Reports of toxicity are rare in horses. Clinical signs occur in 10 to 30 minutes after a toxic dose and may include sweating, ataxia, depression, seizures, and coma. Diagnosis is based on history of exposure to large quantities, clinical signs, and serum and tissue analysis. No specific antidote exists. Treatment is symptomatic, and supportive care is required.

HEAVY METALS: LEAD, IRON

Lead: results from exposure to such lead-containing materials as lead-based paints, putty, caulking compounds, crankcase oils, greases, linoleum, lead solder, roofing materials, asphalt, industrial wastes, discarded automobile batteries, and water from lead plumbing. Young, malnourished animals are more susceptible. High levels of dietary calcium cause decreased absorption of lead from the intestine. Clinical signs are primarily indicative of peripheral-nerve dysfunction and include weakness, loss of coordination, depression, weight loss, paralysis of the throat muscles involved in swallowing and vocalization, loss of proprioception, flaccidity of the rectal sphincter, lip droop, and an inability to chew and swallow normally that may lead to aspiration pneumonia. Lead can cross the placenta, and mares with high lead ingestion may give birth to small, premature, or weak foals. Diagnosis relies on determining blood and/or tissue lead levels. Blood tests screen for blood-cell aminolevulinic acid and porphyrins. Treatment involves eliminating the lead source and administering chelation therapy, typically using calcium disodium EDTA. Additional treatment involves supportive care, particularly for nutrition and hydration. Supplementation of dietary calcium may also be helpful.

Iron: toxicity is usually associated with overdose of oral or injected products or with accidental consumption of iron supplements. Toxicity is least by the oral route. Acute toxicity is associated with death in a few minutes to hours after injection; symptoms resemble an anaphylactic reaction. A progressive form shows depression, jaundice, and disorientation, leading to coma and death. Diagnosis is reached by measuring serum-iron concentrations along with clinical signs and history of iron-supplement administration. Laboratory evidence of liver damage is also common. Treatment of acute cases is unrewarding, as no specific treatment for iron toxicity is known to exist. Supportive care, with consideration for liver function and experimental iron-chelation therapies, may be warranted.

CHAPTER 7
Neuromuscular Disorders

Tetanus is a disease of significant concern to horse owners due to horses' exquisite sensitivity to the tetanus toxin and the common occurrence of the bacterium that produces it, *Clostridium tetani*. The toxin typically gains entry into the body when a wound becomes infected with *Clostridium tetani*. Puncture wounds are especially prone to infection with the bacteria because they are anaerobic, meaning that they survive and replicate only in areas that lack exposure to oxygen. In an anaerobic environment, the bacteria produce the tetanus toxin as they grow and multiply.

Only very small amounts of the tetanus toxin are needed to produce clinical signs in horses. The toxin circulates in the bloodstream and thereby is delivered to the junction of nerves with skeletal muscle. The toxin binds irreversibly to receptors and subsequently migrates to the central nervous system via the nerves. The result is the appearance of uncontrolled and unmitigated effects of the stimulatory nerves only, which manifest as muscle rigidity and spasticity.

Clinical signs of tetanus typically occur between two weeks and one month after bacterial invasion takes place. The first signs may appear only as colic and stiffness of an affected limb. Within 24 hours after the first signs, generalized spasticity is usually evident. An affected animal displays a stiff, stilted gait, an extended head, and a rigid neck. The horse may adopt a "sawhorse" stance. The lips may be retracted, and the ears may be rigid and pulled slightly downward. The tailhead becomes elevated, the muscles become rigid, and the jaws are tightly shut ("lockjaw"). The third eyelid may protrude or prolapse in response to visual stimuli. Sights, sounds, and touch can induce muscle spasms. Severely affected animals may become recumbent. Secondary problems relating to nerve and muscle dysfunction and bacterial infection may occur. As the disease progresses, the horse suffers from increased muscular activity, fever, profuse sweating, inability to swallow, and difficulty breathing. Death occurs from breathing problems and heart failure.

> ## AT A GLANCE
>
> • A horse suffering from tetanus usually displays stiffness, then spasticity.
>
> • Botulism produces weakness and flaccid paralysis.
>
> • Myotonia, which could have a genetic basis, affects skeletal muscle only.
>
> • Hyperkalemic Periodic Paralysis (HYPP) is a muscle cell disorder whose clinical signs can mimic nervous-system dysfunction.

Diagnosis of tetanus is made by clinical signs. The discovery of a wound — especially a puncture wound — supports the diagnosis. Treatment is directed at encouraging muscle relaxation, neutralizing the unbound toxin in the blood, and supportive care. Horses with tetanus should be isolated from visual, sound, and tactile stimuli; a dark, quiet stall is ideal. Muscle relaxants and sedatives may facilitate muscle relaxation and reduced response to external stimuli. The infection site should be opened and cleansed well, and the affected area should be surgically debrided. Penicillin G placement in the wound and systemic administration are useful therapies. Circulating toxin that is yet unbound should be neutralized through the administration of tetanus antitoxin into the muscle. Local infiltration of the wound also may help to neutralize toxin that has not yet entered the blood.

There is some concern regarding a correlation between the administration of tetanus antitoxin and liver disease. Therefore, the utility and necessity of the administration of antitoxin should be weighed against the potential dangers to the liver — which are poorly defined but probably relatively low.

Good supportive care for horses with tetanus includes providing deep bedding, good footing, adequate waste removal, good nutrition, and sufficient hydration. A tetanus toxoid vaccine should be administered along with treatment and boosted four to eight weeks later.

The prognosis for tetanus is guarded. Horses with tetanus exhibit about a 50-percent mortality rate. The rate of progression and severity of clinical signs are indicative of the horse's chances. In general, the more rapid the progression and the more severe the clinical signs, the poorer the prognosis.

To prevent tetanus, administer tetanus toxoid at least once a year following an initial series of vaccinations. Colostral antibodies from the mare may inhibit the development of adequate antibody levels by her foal for six or more months, and mares should be well-vaccinated against tetanus. If the mare's inoculations are current, the newborn foal does not require vaccination with tetanus toxoid or injection of tetanus antitoxin. In fact, newborn foals most likely cannot create protective antibody levels on their own. Furthermore, administering antitoxin could lead to liver failure. It therefore should only be administered if the foal is unprotected, the mare has been poorly vaccinated, and the risk is warranted. Ensuring that the dam is up to date on her tetanus vaccinations is the safest way of imparting maximum immunity levels to her foal.

Foals aged two to six months can be vaccinated with tetanus toxoid and should then be boosted. If the initial vaccination is given at two months of age, boosters should be given at three and six months. If the vaccination is not given until the foal is six months of age, one booster shot given four to six weeks later will suffice.

BOTULISM

Botulism is the result of a toxin produced by the organism *Clostridium botulinum*. Because the botulism toxins are produced by a very similar organism to that which produces tetanus toxin, there are similarities in the mode of exposure to the toxin and the mechanism by which the toxin produces its effects on the nervous system. However, a major difference between botulism and tetanus is that tetanus produces spastic and rigid paralysis, while botulism produces weakness and flaccid paralysis.

Horses are very sensitive to botulism toxin, and clinical signs can be produced by very low — or even undetectable — levels of toxin. Toxin that is absorbed from a wound or from the intestinal tract circulates in the blood. The toxin is believed to block release of the chemicals responsible for the initiation of muscle contraction at the junction of nerves with skeletal and some smooth muscle by binding to sites at these nerve terminals.

. Botulism toxin can enter the body in three ways. One of the most common routes of entry is the ingestion of pre-formed toxin from a contaminated source. Second, ingestion of the *Clostridium botulinum* organism occasionally may lead to production of the toxin in the intestinal tract and its subsequent absorption. Third, a wound may become infected with *Clostridium botulinum* in an anaerobic environment.

Clinical signs of botulism are first noticed one to seven days following the ingestion of or infection with the organism or toxin. If left untreated, botulism is frequently fatal. Clinical signs are often acute in their onset and rapidly progressive. They include diffuse weakness that leads to paralysis and trembling, profound weakness or flaccidity of the tail and anal area, loss of the ability to swallow, salivation, and tongue weakness with inability to retract it when pulled out of the mouth. Other clinical signs may include pupillary dilation, poor gut motility, and inability to urinate.

Some clinical signs may differ with the subtype of the organism; subtypes can produce more than one type of toxin, resulting in slightly variable clinical signs. The likelihood of exposure to a certain subtype varies with geography. Type A toxin is most commonly found west of the Rocky Mountains, type B is common around Kentucky and the mid-Atlantic states, and type C has been documented in Florida. Horses are most sensitive to subtypes B and C of *Clostridium botulinum*.

Clinical signs of botulism produce an index of suspicion, but none of the signs or readily performed laboratory analyses is definitive for the disease. Obtaining a definitive diagnosis requires isolating the toxin from serum, intestinal contents, or feed. Muscle electromyography (EMG) may be helpful in distinguishing botulism from other diseases that are capable of producing similar clinical signs.

Treatment of horses with botulism is primarily symptomatic and supportive. Botulism antitoxin is commercially available from the Michigan Department of Health and tends to be expensive. Antitoxin is not effective at ameliorating clinical signs, as it has no effect on toxin that has already bound to the nerve terminals; it is therefore most helpful in early stages of the disease. Antitoxin may also be useful for neutralizing other circulating, unbound toxin.

Horses with botulism frequently contract secondary bacterial infections. Although prophylactic antibodies are a good idea, one should avoid administering those antibiotics that may exacerbate muscular weakness: aminoglycosides (e.g., gentamicin, amikacin), tetracyclines, and procaine penicillin.

Supportive care is important in treating horses with botulism and should focus on nutrition, hydration, prevention of bacterial infections, minimization of trauma, good footing, and deep bedding. Recumbent horses should be turned frequently. Urinary catheterization is necessary if the horse is unable to urinate on its own. In severe cases, the respiratory muscles become paralyzed, thus interfering with the horse's ability to breathe. Mechanical ventilation has been attempted for some of these horses, but the prognosis is generally poor.

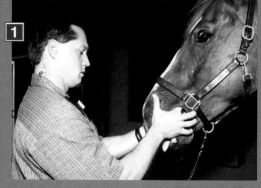

A thorough physical examination (1-3) should precede the neurological exam and may include blood work (4).

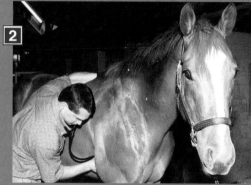

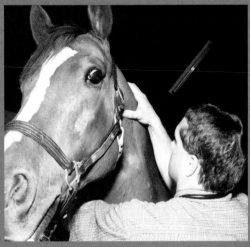

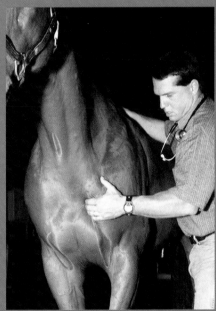

An evaluation of the musculoskeletal system (this page and opposite) may provide clues to neurological abnormalities. Flexibility tests (1&2) are important components of the musculoskeletal exam.

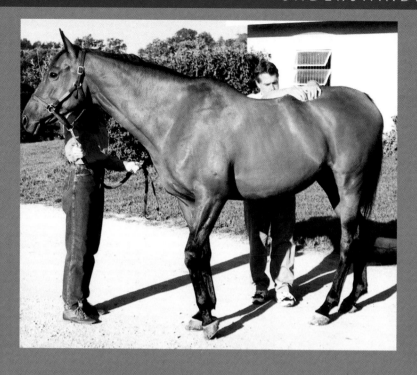

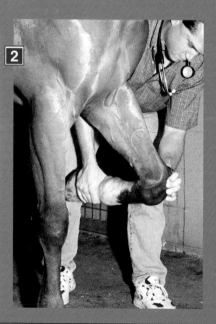

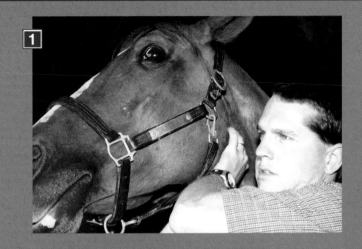

The cranial nerve exam includes checking the glossopharyngeal nerve (1), which controls swallowing, the gag reflex, and taste, and the hypglossal nerve, which controls the tongue (2); and conducting a "menace" test (3) to test the horse's reaction to sudden movement.

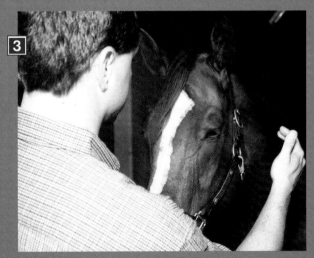

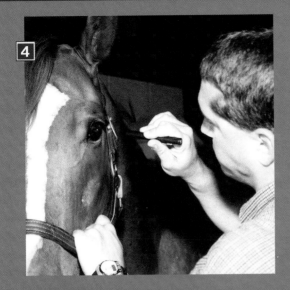

Checking the optic nerve (4), which is responsible for sight, and the trigeminal nerve (5), which provides sensory information from the face and causes movement of the muscles used for chewing.

Placement tests (1&2) help determine if a horse knows where its limbs are; reflex tests (3&4) test responses to certain sensory stimuli.

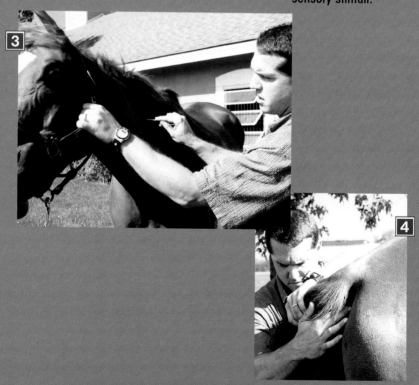

N E U R O L O G I C A L   D I S O R D E R S

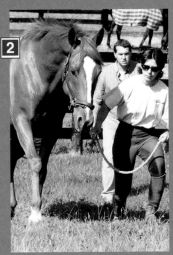

The clinician evaluates the horse's gaits and movement (1) and observes how the horse handles ascending a hill (2); the horse is asked to walk while its head is elevated (3) and to attempt to rebalance itself during a "sway" test (4).

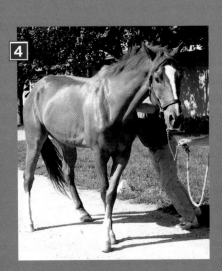

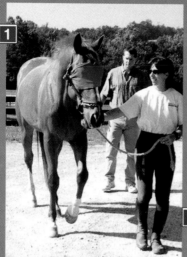

The neurological exam continues with the blindfold test (1), which tests the horse's awareness of limb placement; the tail pull (2), which can reveal weakness in the hindquarters; and turning in tight circles (3), to determine how the horse places its hind legs.

The prognosis for horses with botulism depends on several factors. The amount of toxin present affects the likelihood of recovery; the more toxin present, the poorer the prognosis. Recumbency is a bad sign, as recovery requires the generation of new receptor sites at the nerve terminal and can take weeks. Horses that do not become recumbent may survive with high-quality care. Recovery frequently occurs without significant residual nervous-system deficits. Loss of tail tone and the ability to swallow may be the first signs of the disease to be seen and the last signs to disappear.

It is far better to prevent botulism than to attempt to treat it. Prevention involves eliminating hospitable environments in which the organism can grow. To do so, control vermin populations, dispose of any animal carcasses promptly and appropriately, and avoid purchasing poor-quality feedstuffs. Many farm owners like to feed round bales to horses, but this baling method is conducive to the growth of botulism spores.

Vaccination is only possible against the type B toxin at this time. Anecdotal reports indicate the possibility of a multivalent vaccine in the future. Vaccination of pregnant mares confers protection to the foals as well as the dam. Vaccination of the foal should be initiated at the beginning of the decline of antibodies from the colostrum of the mare, for it has been reported that these antibodies in the foal inhibit the foal from producing its own antibody. Adequate vaccination requires an initial series of three inoculations at one-month intervals, followed by annual boosters.

MYOTONIA

Although this disease is caused by muscle-cell abnormalities, its clinical appearance is similar to that of nervous-system disorders. Myotonia affects skeletal muscle only. Clinical signs frequently begin in the first year and include well-developed musculature and mild pelvic stiffness. Gait abnormalities are most noticeable at the initiation of exercise and become less noticeable as exercise continues.

Stimulation of affected muscles by striking them may produce muscle dimpling in response. Contraction of the muscles may continue for more than 60 seconds.

This disease may have a genetic basis. Horses with myotonia generally do not progress in clinical signs beyond 12 months of age. The disease is diagnosed through the evaluation of the horse's age and through the recognition of clinical signs. Electromyography (EMG) and muscle-biopsy evaluation may aid in reaching a definitive diagnosis.

There is no specific therapy for myotonia. The administration of phenytoin may relieve some symptoms. The prognosis depends on the severity of clinical signs. Some improvement may occur with advancing age. Scar-like tissue may form within the muscles of severely affected horses, leading to persistent pain and difficulty of movement. Consideration of euthanasia in such cases is warranted.

HYPERKALEMIC PERIODIC PARALYSIS (HYPP)

This disease is also caused by muscle-cell disorders, not nervous-system abnormalities. A defect in the way sodium and potassium cross cell membranes causes the symptoms of HYPP. Because the clinical signs may mimic nervous-system disease and because HYPP is relatively common, it has been included in this book. HYPP is of genetic origin: It occurs in Quarter Horses, Paints, Appaloosas, and Quarter Horse crossbreds and has been traced to a common sire, the Quarter Horse stallion Impressive. HYPP is transmitted as a dominant trait and occurs in about 0.4 percent of the Quarter Horse population.

Clinical signs of HYPP vary and are generally more severe in horses that are homozygous for the condition. Homozygous means two identical genetic signals for a particular gene, e.g., two dominant or two recessive. Clinical signs are intermittent and may be induced by certain stimuli. Episodes of clinical signs often begin with muscle contractions and occasionally also a prolapse of the third eyelid.

Sweating and muscle tremors occur, followed by muscle weakness that may progress to recumbency. Heart and respiratory rates may become elevated. Horses that are homozygous may exhibit significant respiratory difficulty due to obstruction of the upper respiratory tract.

Diagnosing HYPP includes taking a pedigree history as well as evaluating the clinical signs. Blood-potassium levels can be measured from blood drawn during an episode; most horses exhibit significantly elevated potassium levels while in the throes of an episode. Researchers have induced episodes experimentally in order to diagnose the condition using orally administered potassium chloride. This test can be dangerous, and appropriate treatment should be readily available during such testing. Genetic testing of whole blood samples reveals whether a horse is HYPP positive and its carrier state (homozygous vs. heterozygous).

Treatment of acute episodes of HYPP involves the administration of dextrose and sodium bicarbonate or calcium gluconate to reduce the levels of potassium in the blood by moving it back into the cells. A tracheotomy may be necessary in cases of severe respiratory distress.

Horse owners can often control the occurrence of HYPP episodes by adjusting their animals' diets to avoid feeds that contain high levels of potassium, such as alfalfa hay, various oil supplements, and sugar and beet molasses. Timothy hay or Bermuda grass, sugar-beet pulp, and grains are appropriate substitutes. Frequent feedings and regular exercise also may reduce the occurrence of episodes. A diuretic drug called acetozolamide has been used with success to help control the occurrence of episodes. The drug is thought to facilitate the elimination of potassium in the urine, thereby controlling episodes.

The prognosis for horses with HYPP is generally favorable. Control measures are usually effective at keeping the episodes at a minimum. Horses with severe clinical signs or that are homozygous may have a less-favorable prognosis. HYPP-positive horses should not be bred.

CHAPTER 8

Nervous-System Disorders of Possible Genetic Origin

OCCIPITOATLANTOAXIAL MALFORMATION (OAAM)

At least five types of malformations of the bony spinal column in the area in which it joins the skull (the occipitoatlantoaxial joints) exist. These conditions are heritable in Arabians, but also are seen in Quarter Horses, Morgans, and possibly other breeds.

Bone malformations typically cause nervous-system derangement due to effects on the brainstem and/or spinal cord. Typical clinical signs include partial paralysis of all four legs shortly after birth, with progression to complete paralysis at variable rates. Signs of nervous-system deficits are often symmetric. Occasionally, affected horses may not show nervous-system abnormalities until they are few years old. An affected horse may be reluctant to move its neck, may exhibit a twisting of the neck, or may hold the head extended.

Diagnosis is made by examining radiographs of the neck and by identifying malformation of the affected bones. Surgical fusion of the joints with spinal-cord decompression is a potential treatment. However, due to the high heritability of the disease, affected Arabian horses should not be treated. Severe nervous-system derangement is not successfully controlled with medications alone. Therefore, in cases in which surgical intervention is impractical or unwarranted, euthanasia is appropriate.

CERVICAL COMPRESSIVE MYELOPATHY (CCM-"WOBBLERS")

Whether this disease is of genetic origin is unclear, but researchers believe that other conditions must also be present in order for a horse to become a "wobbler." Certain breeds, such as Thoroughbreds, may produce a greater-than-normal proportion of wobblers. However, the ways in which these horses are fed and handled may well contribute to the process. CCM is typically identified in

> ## AT A GLANCE
>
> • At least five types of bone malformations are heritable in Arabians and some other breeds.
>
> • A "wobbler" usually shows symptoms from ages one to three. Clinical signs include ataxia, spasticity, knuckling, and stumbling.
>
> • Narcolepsy is a rare and incurable sleep disorder characterized by sudden loss of muscle tone and initiation of sleep.

horses from one to three years of age, but it has been identified in horses as old as 10.

CCM can manifest as one of two types of spinal-cord compression. In the first, the spinal canal narrows through the bones of the vertebrae, potentially producing persistent clinical signs of spinal-cord deficits. This type is commonly identified at the C5 to C7 vertebrae. The second type, dynamic compression, is also referred to as cervical vertebral instability. The compression is described as dynamic because it most often manifests when the neck is flexed. Dynamic compression most often occurs at sites C3 to C5.

Clinical signs of wobblers syndrome include ataxia — which is often worse in the hind limbs than it is in the forelimbs — spasticity, knuckling, stumbling, swinging of the limbs far away from the body when the horse is turned in a circle, pelvic sway, a poor-quality trot or walk, a reluctance to move backward and to bend the neck, and poor limb-replacement reflexes.

Diagnosis of CCM involves obtaining high-quality radiographs of the cervical spinal column and taking various measurements to determine the likelihood of a compressive site. Sites of bony change on X-rays may indicate areas of previous trauma or instability. Although the applied measurements can be helpful in reaching a tentative diagnosis, they cannot conclusively predict sites of spinal-cord compression. Myelography can produce more conclusive evidence of cord compression. In this procedure, which requires general anesthesia, a dye that is visible on radiographs is injected into the space around the spinal cord. Abnormal horses are believed to have greater than 50 percent narrowing of the dye columns at affected sites. Side effects relating to the injection of the dye or to general anesthesia are possible but are uncommon and are generally mild if they occur.

Some horses with CCM can be treated. Younger horses tend to have a better chance of improvement, but no universally successful treatment exists. Corticosteroids may help control clinical signs, but they generally do not lead to long-term resolution of nervous deficits.

Some cases have been treated surgically to fuse or decompress the affected joints, but complications from surgical intervention are possible. A highly caloric-restrictive diet may alleviate symptoms in young horses, but such diets must be formulated carefully so that they do not compromise horses' nutritional needs. Some success has been reported with the use of strict stall confinement as a treatment, but early detection and intervention are necessary. Severely neurologic horses are dangerous to themselves and to others, and in such cases euthanasia should be considered. Prognosis for athletic performance is directly related to severity of clinical signs. Horses with significant nervous system deficits should not be ridden.

NIGHT BLINDNESS

Night blindness is a disease of Appaloosa horses that affects the retina. The condition affects the animal's vision, and the severity varies. Clinical signs range from mild vision impairment to complete blindness in the dark, apprehension in daylight, and abnormal pupil shapes and movement. Diagnosis is made by considering the horse's history, breed, clinical signs, and by using a maze to test its vision and reactions in light and dark environments. Electrical testing of the retina (electroretinography) can produce a definitive diagnosis. Examination of the retina using an ophthalmoscope usually yields normal findings. There is no treatment for this disorder.

NARCOLEPSY

This is a rare and incurable sleep disorder characterized by sudden loss of muscle tone and initiation of sleep. It has been documented in several breeds, including Welsh ponies, miniature horses, Thoroughbreds, Quarter Horses, Morgans, Appaloosas, and Standardbreds. A biochemical abnormality in the sleep-wake center of the central nervous system may accompany this disease. Episodes of muscle weakness may cause affected horses to fall (cataplexy); certain events, such as being patted, led out of a stall, eating, or drinking, may precipitate the episodes.

Clinical signs of narcolepsy include mild muscle weakness to complete collapse and falling to the knees or stumbling, exhibition of REM sleep, and episodes that last a few seconds to 10 minutes. Affected horses appear to be normal between attacks.

In diagnosing narcolepsy, the clinician should rule out other possible causes. The CSF of affected horses is normal. The brain waves of horses experiencing an attack show the brain activity of REM sleep. To test the brain waves of a suspected narcoleptic horse, the clinician can induce an episode by administering physostigmine into the vein. The episode usually begins three to 10 minutes later. Atropine can be used to control the severity of the episodes and may help to prevent recurrence of attacks.

Treatment of narcolepsy is attempted by administering an antidepressant drug called imipramine. Oral administration produces variable results. Atropine can help to control the occurrence of episodes for up to 30 hours.

The prognosis of horses with narcolepsy is variable. Some young horses recover completely from the disease. Other horses — especially those in which the disorder commenced during their adult lives — continue to experience episodes throughout their lives.

NEURAXONAL DYSTROPHY

This disease has been described as a separate nervous-system disease in Morgans and possibly Arabians and appears to be transmitted genetically. The specific cause of the nervous-system abnormality is not well defined. The condition is irreversible and is characterized by loss of coordination or stiffness of the hind limbs. The forelimbs are affected in only the most severe cases. The disease may appear similar to EDM (see Chapter 10) in both clinical signs and post-mortem findings, although foreleg involvement is more commonly seen with EDM.

Neuraxonal dystrophy is diagnosed through an evaluation of the horse's breed and of its clinical signs. Definitive diagnosis is made by post-mortem examination. Treatment is symptomatic and may require nonspecific treatments such as vitamin E supplementation and glucocorticoids. The disease can be severe and progressive. Debilitation may require consideration of euthanasia.

CEREBELLAR ABIOTROPHY AND DEGENERATION

Abiotrophy refers to the premature degeneration of nerves due to an intrinsic abnormality in structure or metabolism. This disease is likely of genetic origin. Cerebellar abiotrophy has been reported in Arabians, Gotland ponies, and Oldenburgs. Degenerative cerebellar disease also has been reported in Thoroughbred and Paso Fino foals. Arabians and part-Arabians are the most commonly affected breeds in North America. The disorder is generally seen in foals under one year of age. A foal may be born normal and develop clinical signs sometime thereafter.

Clinical signs include head tremor, ataxia, abnormal stance and gait, and spasticity of the limbs. Diagnosis is by recognition of clinical signs and breed. Ancillary tests are of little help. Treatment of this disease is not effective.

CHAPTER 9

Disorders Related to Metabolism and Organ Dysfunction

HEPATIC ENCEPHALOPATHY

As the name implies, this disorder is associated with severe liver (hepatic) insufficiency or failure. The clinical signs are variable and range from mild changes in behavior, irritability, ataxia, persistent yawning, and aimless walking to more severe behavior changes, drowsiness, aggressive behavior, recumbency, seizures, and coma.

In cases of hepatic encephalopathy, the central nervous system becomes deranged as a result of poorly functioning liver cells. One explanation is that the liver becomes less efficient at neutralizing and removing potential neurotoxins that occur naturally or accumulate in the presence of liver insufficiency. Because the liver plays a significant role in detoxifying ammonia — a byproduct of the body's process of protein degradation — ammonia has received much attention in the role of development of the disease. However, although horses with liver disease and hepatic encephalopathy frequently exhibit elevated ammonia levels, some horses with hepatic encephalopathy do not have elevated ammonia levels. Therefore, other toxins and factors, including such other neurotransmitter molecules as GABA, may be associated with the development of hepatic encephalopathy.

A diagnosis of hepatic encephalopathy is based on neurologic signs of cerebral dysfunction, along with a physical examination and laboratory findings that are indicative of liver disease. Other possible diagnoses should be excluded, as none of the clinical signs of hepatic encephalopathy is specific to the condition.

Treatment of hepatic encephalopathy involves supportive care and specific

> ## AT A GLANCE
>
> • Liver dysfunction or failure can cause neurological dysfunction.
>
> • Clinical signs of low blood sugar can include trembling, ataxia, and seizures.
>
> • Potassium and calcium deficiencies can lead to nervous-system abnormalities.

treatment of the underlying liver disease. If severe nervous-system signs are present, sedation and seizure control may be necessary. The prognosis depends on the severity of the underlying disease. Signs of encephalopathy may be reversible if liver disease is controllable and if seizures, coma, head-pressing, or other signs of advanced disease are not present. In cases of severe, acute liver failure and severe nervous-system derangement, euthanasia should be considered. Horses that are euthanized and do not have a definitive diagnosis should be considered potential rabies cases.

HYPOGLYCEMIA

Hypoglycemia (low blood sugar) is infrequently encountered in horses. Septicemia, liver insufficiency, or an insulin-producing tumor could produce signs of hypoglycemia.

Clinical signs of low blood glucose may include trembling, ataxia, increased heart and respiratory rates, pupillary dilation, sweating, nystagmus progressing to recumbency, seizures, coma, and death.

Diagnosis of hypoglycemia involves testing the horse's blood-glucose levels. The clinician should consider any underlying conditions that may have caused or contributed to the condition.

Treatment of hypoglycemia involves administering intravenous glucose or simply by feeding smaller and more frequent amounts if signs are not severe and intestinal function is normal.

ABNORMAL BLOOD-POTASSIUM LEVELS

Potassium has important effects on nerve and heart-muscle function. Potassium is absorbed by the intestine and is found in fluid outside of the body's cells (extracellular fluid), but is highest in concentration inside cells (intracellular fluid). Blood levels of potassium are regulated by release and uptake from cells, and by elimination, conservation balance by the kidneys, and dietary intake.

Low blood potassium, which can lead to nervous-system abnormalities, can be caused by chronic kidney disease, intestinal disease, inadequate potassium intake, potassium loss, insulin or glucose overadministration, or acid/base abnormalities. Low blood potassium manifests as muscle weakness.

High blood-potassium levels are associated with such diseases as acute kidney failure, ruptured bladder, HYPP, severe tissue damage, blood cell lysis, acid/base problems, cardiac-rhythm disturbances, and hormonal problems. As in cases of HYPP, muscle weakness may be a symptom.

ABNORMAL BLOOD-CALCIUM LEVELS

Low blood-calcium levels are more common than high blood-calcium levels. Blood calcium exists in both a protein-bound state and as free ionized calcium. Both states are quantifiable by laboratory testing. Depressed blood-calcium levels may occur in association with severe, prolonged exercise; insufficient dietary calcium; lactation; pregnancy; or transport. Clinical signs in horses can include muscle cramping, tetany, thumps (synchronous diaphragmatic flutter), poor intestinal motility, and weak heart contractions or arrhythmias.

Chronic kidney failure, excessive supplementation, and some tumors and intoxications can lead to elevated blood-calcium levels, which can affect the heart and even can lead to cardiac arrest.

ABNORMAL BLOOD-SODIUM LEVELS

Nervous-system abnormalities may result from an excess of blood sodium, but abnormally high levels are uncommon in horses. Rapid overingestion, overadministration of sodium chloride-containing products, and water deprivation may lead to elevated blood sodium. Clinical signs include diarrhea, blindness, stargazing, hyperexcitability, ataxia, proprioceptive deficits, head-pressing, chewing, rapid, involuntary eyeball movement, muscle-twitching, and death. Slow correction of the high sodium levels — including control of oral water intake — is necessary to prevent nervous-system signs. Control of cerebral-edema formation during rehydration also is necessary.

Horses with diarrhea, blood loss, excessive sweating, hormonal imbalances, or ruptured bladder (in foals) may have depressed blood-sodium levels. The danger to the central nervous system is not the low sodium level itself, but rather the rapidity of the correction of the low levels. Cerebral edema during correction of sodium levels is best controlled by administering sodium-containing fluids at a controlled and monitored rate. The fluids used should have a concentration of sodium similar to that of the normal body concentration of sodium.

THIAMINE DEFICIENCY

Horses whose diets contain enzymes that can break down thiamine can develop thiamine deficiency. The plants bracken fern and horsetail, and the anticoccidial drug amprolium (commonly given to cattle) all contain such enzymes. Clinical signs of thiamine deficiency include ataxia, proprioceptive deficits, depressed heart rate, blindness, abnormal urination, and muscle tremors. The deficiency is diagnosed through history and clinical signs. Treatment with intravenous thiamine is effective.

CHAPTER 10

Nervous-System Disorders of Poorly Defined Causes

POLYNEURITIS EQUI

Polyneuritis equi is relatively uncommon and has no known cause. Immune-mediated causes and inflammatory disease related to viral infections have been suggested but so far remain unsubstantiated. Early clinical signs may involve hyperreactivity to stimulation of the skin on and around the head and the area between the hind legs surrounding the anus (the perineum). Chronic cases exhibit paralysis of the tail, anus, rectum, and bladder. Cranial-nerve deficits may occur along with these signs. Ataxia of the fore- or hind limbs may be present, and the gluteal muscles and areas supplied by affected cranial nerves may atrophy. Colic may occur as a result of fecal retention due to a flaccid anal sphincter. The disease often affects bladder function, resulting in urinary incontinence and retention.

A definitive diagnosis of polyneuritis equi is possible only with a post-mortem examination. Blood work may reveal evidence of a chronic inflammatory process. Cerebrospinal-fluid examination may show increases in the protein concentration, with or without an accompanying increase in the white-cell count. The presence of the P2 myelin antibody in the serum of CSF may be supportive of the diagnosis.

Treatment of polyneuritis equi is nonspecific. Supportive therapy is essential and should focus on assisting such failing body functions as defecation and urination. Secondary infections, such as bacterial cystitis (commonly associated with bladder dysfunction), may occur and should be treated with antimicrobial drugs. Corticosteroids may be useful but typically produce only moderate, short-term effects. Despite a slow disease progression, the long-term prognosis is generally poor.

AT A GLANCE

- Some breeds appear susceptible to diseases such as EDM and EMND.

- Stringhalt is recognized as excessive flexion of one or both hind limbs.

- Draft breeds can suffer from shivers — muscle tremors of the hind limbs and tail.

EQUINE DEGENERATIVE MYELOENCEPHALOPATHY (EDM)

EDM is a disease that affects the spinal cord, primarily in young horses. A familial tendency has been suggested in the Paso Fino, Arabian, Appaloosa, and Thoroughbred breeds; however, no pattern of inheritance has been identified. Clinical signs of EDM are often noticed in horses less than a year old, but also are seen in horses several years of age. The onset of symptoms may be abrupt or slow.

Clinical signs of EDM include ataxia, proprioceptive deficits, weakness, and spasticity of all four limbs, with the hind limbs often being the most affected. An affected horse may exhibit a "stabbing" gait and may drag its toes. It resists backing and may drag its feet or assume a "dog-sitting" position. When turned in a tight circle, it will pivot on the inside limb and swing the outside limb out away from its body. It is also prone to falling.

The cause of EDM is poorly defined. The disease has often been associated with vitamin E deficiency. Hereditary factors and toxic compounds also may play a role in the development of EDM.

EDM is diagnosed through microscopic examination of the spinal cord. The ante-mortem diagnosis relies on history, clinical signs, and the elimination of other diseases as possible causes. Low-serum vitamin E levels in horses with compatible clinical signs and good diagnostic evaluations are supportive of an EDM diagnosis.

Treatment of EDM is nonspecific. Affected horses have been reported to benefit from vitamin E supplements. Earlier treatment with vitamin E is more likely to be helpful. Horses kept on sand or dirt lots may be at greater risk for this disease. High-quality forage and vitamin E supplementation may be advisable for horses with low vitamin E levels or vitamin E-poor diets.

EQUINE MOTOR NEURON DISEASE (EMND)

Most documented cases of EMND have occurred in the northeastern United States. Many breeds appear to be affected, but the majority have been Quarter Horses.

Early signs of EMND include muscle tremors, frequent shifts of weight, and recumbency. An affected horse may

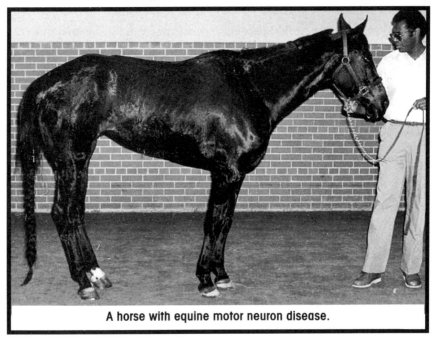

A horse with equine motor neuron disease.

stand with all four legs close together and under the body. The gait appears short-strided but not ataxic. Loss of proprioception does not appear to occur. Later in the disease progression, an affected horse loses weight and muscle mass — particularly in the scapula, triceps, quadriceps, and neck muscles — and may be unable to hold its head up. Loss of nerve supply to the sacrodorsalis medialis coccygeal muscle may result in elevated tail carriage. The retina may show a characteristic pigment accumulation. The disease progression may take several months.

Ante-mortem diagnosis can be difficult but is supported by clinically compatible signs and elevation in serum-muscle enzyme levels. A biopsy of the sacrodorsalis medialis coccygeal muscle may provide microscopic evidence of the disease. An experienced neuropathologist may be able to make a definitive ante-mortem diagnosis by examining a biopsy of the spinal accessory nerve under a microscope.

The cause of EMND consistently is linked to low levels of vitamin E and superoxide dismutase but are probably not the sole causes. A significant association has been identified among increased levels of copper in the tissues of the central nervous system, increased levels of iron in the liver, and EMND. Lack of pasture also appears to be a risk factor in the development of EMND.

Treatment of EMND is based on symptomatic and supportive care as well as on minimizing associated risk factors. Horses with little or no pasture or hay should be tested for vitamin E levels and supplemented as needed.

EQUINE DYSAUTONOMIA (GRASS SICKNESS)

This disease is most common in the United Kingdom and in northern Europe. Most clinical signs relate to poor intestinal motility: colic, abdominal distention, weight loss, poor appetite, and insufficient hydration. Some cases may experience urinary-bladder paralysis. Death can be rapid, or the disease process may be protracted.

The cause of the disease is unknown, but affected horses display a degeneration of those parts of the nervous system that govern intestinal motility. A toxic factor has been suggested as a possible cause. Diagnosis of the disease relies on the history and clinical signs, with supportive tests indicating poor intestinal motility. A definitive diagnosis can be made only at post-mortem.

Treatment of equine dysautonomia is supportive and includes supplemental feeding and fluid therapies. The disease prognosis is generally poor. A limited number of chronically affected horses have recovered.

STRINGHALT

This condition is recognized as excessive flexion of one or both hind limbs. Signs may be worse on turning and backing and in cold weather.

No known specific cause of stringhalt exists. Underlying conditions that may cause the disorder include sensory-nerve disorders, muscle disorders, or spinal-cord disease. The typical gait may be explained by other nervous-system or musculoskeletal disorders. Such disorders should be ruled out by complete diagnostic evaluation before the clinician concludes that a horse suffers from primary stringhalt. Unfortunately, no specific diagnostic test for stringhalt exists.

Stringhalt is treated by surgical sectioning of the lateral digital extensor tendon. Some horses may improve with the administration of oral phenytoin. More conservative approaches are advised before resorting to surgery.

SHIVERS AND SIMILAR DISORDERS

Typically identified in draft breeds, shivers produces muscle tremors of the hind limbs and tail that occur when the affected horse moves — especially when asked to back. Exaggerated flexion and outward movement of one or both hind limbs may occur; the forelimbs are less commonly involved. Shivers and similar disorders often are progressive.

These types of conditions have been described as peripheral-nerve disorders, but more recent evidence may point to a primary muscle abnormality. Recently, a primary muscle disorder called glycogen storage myopathy has been investigated and well outlined. The clinical signs are similar to those described above. Muscle biopsy and biochemical analysis have proven to be helpful in its analysis. Although no specific diagnostic tests exist, serum-muscle enzymes may be elevated, and post-mortem microscopic examination of the involved muscle may be helpful. Feeding a high-fat, low-carbohydrate diet may help control the condition.

CHAPTER 11

Space-Occupying Lesions of the Nervous System and Other Conditions

ABSCESSES

Abscesses can cause nervous-system abnormalities when they occur in the nervous system. Brain abscesses have been documented in association with *Streptococcus equi* infections. Abscessation of the pituitary gland also has been described. Any abscess in or associated with nervous-system tissue may break open and seed the nervous system with its inflammatory or bacterial contents, often resulting in the development of meningitis.

The presence of an abscess in or associated with nervous-system tissue may cause nervous-system abnormalities as a result of local compression or nerve inflammation. The location of the abscess determines the resulting clinical signs. Treatment usually involves the appropriate administration of antimicrobials, anti-inflammatory agents, and supportive care.

TUMORS

Tumors of the nervous system are uncommon. Primary nervous-system tumors are even more uncommon. Lymphosarcoma may be the most commonly identified tumor in the equine central nervous system and usually is the result of metastasis from another site. Some more commonly identified tumors and tumor-like masses are cholesteatomas in the brain and pituitary-gland tumors. Tumors in the central nervous system may cause signs varying from severe behavioral changes to mild ataxia and proprioceptive deficits. Peripheral-nerve tumors or tumors of other tissue types that affect peripheral nerves will manifest clinical signs that relate to the affected nerves.

> ## AT A GLANCE
>
> - Tumors and abscesses can cause nervous-system abnormalities when they occur in the nervous system.
>
> - Some "dummy" foals can suffer neurologic damage.
>
> - Infection of the spinal bones occurs mainly in foals and young horses.

GRANULOMAS

A granuloma is a space-occupying mass that is similar in character to an abscess. However, granulomas tend to be created from a more chronic process. Granulomas may also harbor infectious agents. Their major effect is produced by local compression and inflammation of nearby nerves. Clinical signs associated with granulomas in the nervous system depend on the location of the affected nerves or nerve tracts. Treatment of such conditions involves the administration of anti-inflammatory agents and antimicrobials if an infectious agent is suspected.

OTHER CONDITIONS THAT AFFECT THE NERVOUS SYSTEM

Lightning Strike

Nervous system abnormalities may be only one manifestation of lightning strike in horses. Lightning strike appears to be frequently fatal in horses. In addition to nervous system abnormalities, cardiac, circulatory, musculoskeletal, optic, and dermal abnormalities may be seen.

Affected horses are often found or located in an environment conducive to lightning strike. Such areas include under tall trees, open fields, near underground wires or in a shelter without a lightning rod system.

Clinical signs and physical findings indicative of lightning strike include singeing of hair or burns, bleeding from the ear, mouth, or nose, protruding anus, and fetal expulsion in pregnant mares. Clinical laboratory findings may show muscle damage from severe contractions and thermal, mechanical or electrical energy damage. Post-mortem examination findings may produce other findings indicative of lightning strike including congested viscera and veins, necrosis of the middle and internal ear, contracted heart, and bone fractures. Failure to find other causes of sudden death is supportive of lightning strike.

Neurologic impairment is variable. Acute rapid death may result from direct strike and/or strike to the head. A common neurologic syndrome appears to be related to unilateral vestibular disease. Depression, loss of consciousness, hyperexcitability, recumbency, paralysis, impaired vision, vertigo, rapid, involuntary eyeball movement, and deafness are possible findings associated with lightning strike.

Muscle damage may appear as stiff gait with pain and swelling over the affected area.

Treatment of lightning strike involves emergency procedures and central nervous system anti-inflammatory and anti-edema therapy, antibiotics for potential secondary bacterial infection, good supportive care, and treatment of secondary conditions such as corneal ulceration or wound management.

Prevention of lightning strike involves protection from lightning in appropriately designed structures. Avoidance of turn-out in open fields/paddocks and sheltering under tall trees is prudent.

Fibrocartilaginous Embolization

This condition has been described only to a very limited

extent. The material that becomes free probably enters the vessels that supply certain regions of the central nervous system. Clogging of the arteries then leads to swelling, bleeding, and loss of oxygen supply to the affected areas. The emboli (material that enters the vessels and then clogs them) occur in the brain, the spinal cord, and the cerebellum.

Clinical signs may include sudden partial paralysis of the limbs, exaggerated limb reflexes below the site of embolization, or an absence of reflex responses in the area of the peripheral nervous system containing the lesion. Other signs may relate to affected upper areas of the central nervous system.

Treatment of this condition involves good supportive care and nonspecific anti-inflammatory therapy. Early identification of this problem might facilitate other useful therapies, but is very difficult using the diagnostic modalities available today for use in horses.

Headshaking

There are a number of possible explanations for headshaking in horses. Some of these are tooth problems or an abscessed root of a tooth, inflammatory or allergic conditions relating to the nose or nasal cavity, ocular abnormalities, ocular vitreous chamber floaters, otitis media/interna, otitis externa, ear mites and other parasites, neck injury, cranial-nerve dysfunction, guttural-pouch diseases, and unknown causes.

Diagnosis of headshaking in the horse should take into account the myriad of possible causes. In a limited number of cases, blocking the trigeminal nerve has assisted in diagnosing the cause of the disorder. Indeed, trigeminal neurectomy has been performed in a few horses to treat persistent headshaking. However, severe complications are possible with this surgery, and the procedure should be performed only by well-qualified surgeons and only after all other therapeutic options have been exhausted and following extensive discussion by qualified clinicians.

More recently, a light-triggered equine headshaking syndrome has been documented. The onset of clinical signs tends to be in the spring and may be related to the hours of daylight. The stimulation of a sneeze response in humans as a result of exposure of the face to direct sunlight may be triggered by a similar mechanism to that which triggers headshaking in horses with this disorder. Clinical signs begin when an affected horse is taken outdoors.

Headshaking can be stopped by the application of blindfolds or dark lenses. Signs improve with the reduction of light and are absent at night. Many horses improve with the oral administration of cyproheptadine. Headshaking tends to return in 24 hours after treatment ceases.

Hypoxic Ischemic Encephalopathy
(Neonatal Maladjustment Syndrome)

"Dummy foal" syndrome is a noninfectious disorder of newborn foals that is associated with a period of insufficient oxygen supply — often so short as to go unnoticed — before, during, or shortly after birth. Poor central-nervous-system oxygenation may lead to damage to or even death of nerve cells in the central nervous system. Affected areas may suffer edema or hemorrhage; and disorders of the brain, brainstem, and spinal cord may result.

Clinical signs relate to the areas and extent of inflammation and are more severe with longer periods of poor oxygenation. The most severe cases may result in coma and death. Less-severe signs can include seizures, behavioral abnormalities, poor respiration, inability to nurse (possibly resulting in aspiration pneumonia), decreased awareness of surroundings, stupor, intermittent periods of unresponsiveness, ataxia, cranial-nerve deficits, poor or absent reflexes, or exaggerated reflexes.

Diagnosis involves knowledge of the history and the presence of compatible clinical signs. The disorder cannot be diagnosed using laboratory tests. Some clinicians recommend using electrodiagnostics such as EEG (electroencephalography) or auditory-evoked response testing to assist in diagnosing this condition. Definitive diagnosis is made by post-mortem examination of affected areas of the central nervous system.

Neurologic impairment is possible — if not probable — but may be difficult to document after an affected foal

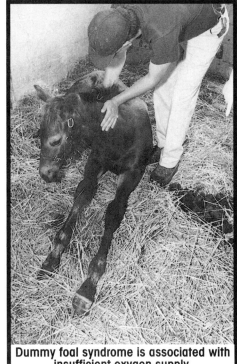

Dummy foal syndrome is associated with insufficient oxygen supply.

has matured. Treatment is primarily supportive and focuses on controlling seizures, providing adequate nutrition, maintaining a proper acid/base balance, providing respiratory support, and using anti-inflammatory and other agents judiciously to control edema and hemorrhage. About half the foals with this syndrome recover to become mature and clinically normal adults.

Neuromas

The development of a neuroma is usually associated with surgical procedures performed on peripheral nerves. The most common site for a neuroma is the back of the pastern of a foreleg after a posterior digital neurectomy ("nerving"). Fibers from the transected nerve resprout, producing a "nest" at the end of the nerve that can become painful to the touch and cause lameness. Painful neuromas of the trigeminal nerve have occurred after neurectomy to control headshaking. This is considered to be a potential complication of this type of surgery and does not occur in the majority of cases.

A procedure called neural capping can help to prevent the development of neuromas. If a neuroma does indeed develop, the original surgical procedure usually must be repeated. Conservative medical management of neuromas using long-term blocking agents and steroids is difficult and usually does not produce long-term success. Neuromas of the trigeminal nerve are difficult to correct surgically. The pain is exquisite in such cases, and some horses have required euthanasia.

Osteomyelitis/Discospondylitis

This condition involves infection of the bone(s) of the spinal column and is most common in young horses or foals. The infectious agent is usually bacteria; fungal infections are rare. *Rhodococcus equi*, *Salmonella* species, and *Actinobacillus equuli* are common causes in foals; *Brucella abortis* and *Mycobacterium tuberculosis* are more often seen in adult cases.

Infection of the spinal bones may be associated with neonatal septicemia in foals and with immunosuppression, infection, and trauma in young and adult horses. Clinical signs can include acute pain and stiffness, with evidence of spinal-cord compression. Heat, pain, and swelling may be the only clinical signs, but other cases may present with the evidence of spinal-cord compression relating to the location of the bone infection. Such signs may include either exaggerated or poor reflexes and patches of sweating.

Diagnosis of this condition may require several types of tests. A history of a concurrent infection elsewhere in the body can increase the index of suspicion for this condition, particularly in cases of newborn foals and of horses that are immunosuppressed. Spinal radiographs can provide good evidence of the condition. However, radiographic changes may not be immediately apparent. Cerebrospinal-fluid evaluation may or may not be helpful. Only rarely can the organism be cultured from the CSF; and changes in it, when present, are usually compatible with compression of the spinal cord. Newer diagnostic modalities may be much more helpful in localizing and diagnosing the condition. These include ultra-sound, thermography, and nuclear scintigraphy. Newborn foals with this condition should receive blood cultures, as the origin of the infection may well be neonatal septicemia. Direct aspiration of the infected bone has been utilized for diagnosis and to guide antimicrobial therapy.

Treatment involves administering appropriate antimicrobial agents, preferably based on the results of a culture. Anti-inflammatory therapies can be used to ease pain, fever, and inflammation. Surgical intervention may be considered in cases requiring drainage and spinal-cord decompression, but the cost of such procedures should be carefully considered in relation to the likelihood of a successful outcome. The overall prognosis depends on early detection, the ability to provide and sustain appropriate therapy, and the severity of infection and spinal-cord compression.

Intracarotid Drug Injection

Inadvertent administration of many commonly used medications into the carotid artery can produce serious acute neurologic reactions. Such compounds may include xylazine (Rompun), flunixin meglumine (Banamine), phenylbutazone (Bute), other tranquilizers, calcium solutions, and sodium iodide. Any medication injected into the carotid artery has the potential — if not the likelihood — to produce an unwanted reaction.

The reaction most often occurs as a result of the administration into the carotid artery of a substance meant to be administered into the jugular vein. It may be more commonly encountered when injections are given in the lower two-thirds of the neck, where the jugular vein and the carotid artery lie next to each other. To help protect against intracarotid injections, give IV injections only in the upper third of the neck, where the jugular vein is separated from the carotid artery by a muscle called the omohyoideus. However, even in this location, intracarotid injection is possible. IV medications should be administered only by people who have been taught how to give them properly.

The condition is marked by a neurologic reaction that takes place immediately after an attempted IV injection. Typically, the animal rears and falls over backward. Seizure-like activity often ensues. Some animals die; others recover completely. Some horses that recover may suffer residual nervous-system damage, including blindness, head tilt, and proprioceptive deficits. Occasionally, signs of Horner's syndrome (see Chapter 6) may occur when the sympathetic nerve trunk is damaged.

There is no effective treatment for this condition. Violent horses require a safe environment and sedation. Administration of glucocorticoids and other medications to help control central-nervous-system edema or hemorrhage may be helpful.

Seizures/Convulsions

Adult horses have a relatively high threshold for seizures; foals have a much lower seizure threshold. When they occur, seizures can be partial, generalized, or status epilepticus. Partial seizures result in localized clinical signs such as twitching of the face or limbs. A generalized seizure involves the entire area of the cerebral cortex and results in generalized muscle activity over the entire body and loss of consciousness. Status epilepticus is the recurrence of generalized seizures in rapid succession. It is believed to be uncommon in horses.

The most common cause of seizures in newborn foals is hypoxic ischemic encephalopathy (NMS, "dummy foal" syndrome), trauma, or meningitis. Foals under one year of age are most commonly affected by trauma or epilepsy from unknown causes. Seizures in adult horses most commonly are caused by trauma, hepatoencephalopathy, tumors, and various toxicities.

Diagnosis of seizures relies on clinical signs. The extent of cerebral involvement determines the clinical manifestation of the seizure. Partial seizures may include twitching of a muscle group or limb, chewing, compulsive running or walking, and self-mutilation. Generalized seizures may occur after an initial period of uneasiness (aura), followed by symmetric muscle contraction and relaxation that may lead to recumbency and loss of consciousness. Other signs may include deviation of the eyeballs, salivation, "stargazing," paddling of the limbs, urination, defecation, and sweating. Generalized seizures may last up to a minute. Narcolepsy and HYPP can be easily confused with seizures.

Skull X-rays, nuclear scintigraphy, CT scans, or MRI imaging may help to determine the presence of a skull fracture or neurologic abnormality. CSF analysis may also provide useful information in determining the cause of the seizures. Electroencephalography (EEG) can be used to help determine the location and cause of the seizures.

Treatment of seizures is aimed at controlling their severity and frequency. Underlying conditions should be addressed and treated when possible. Anti-seizure drugs may be required on an acute or a long-term basis. Medications used in the acute phase of seizure control include diazepam (valium), pentobarbital, chloral hydrate, and other similar drugs. Nonspecific therapies are often included in acute treatment and can include corticosteroids or other anti-inflammatory agents. Long-term treatment usually involves the use of phenobarbital or phenytoin.

The prognosis for a horse suffering from seizures depends on the success of therapies used to eliminate the causes of the seizures, the severity of the seizures themselves, and the horse's response to those medications used to control them.

Peripheral Motor or Sensory Deficits Due to Recumbency and Anesthesia

Due to horses' large size, peripheral motor and/or sensory deficits can occur in association with prolonged recumbency resulting from illness or general anesthesia. Body weight plays a significant role in two ways. First, prolonged compromise of the blood supply to an area may occur due to compression of vessels on the animal's down side. Second, prolonged compression of local nerves may produce inflammation and subsequent derangement in nerve function in downside areas subjected to compression by body weight.

Muscle damage often accompanies prolonged recumbency due to inhibited blood supply and physical damage of muscle tissue. Therefore, any disease or condition that causes recumbency can produce this type of muscle damage. Muscle damage due to recumbency can lead to severe inflammation and altered sensory function in the area. These problems may be difficult to distinguish from primary nerve damage caused by trauma.

Nerve damage is produced by the same mechanism as muscle damage. Physical compression of nerves may cause significant edema, inflammation, and nerve dysfunction. Blood supply to these nerves also may be affected.

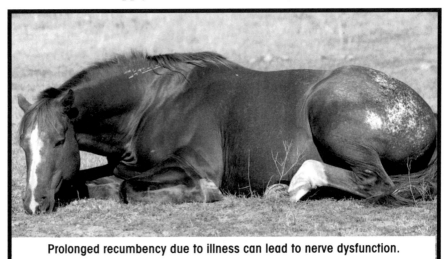

Prolonged recumbency due to illness can lead to nerve dysfunction.

Clinical manifestations of this type of nerve damage relate to the nerve(s) affected. Commonly affected nerves include the ulnar or radial nerve or their branches of the front legs, and the femoral and sciatic or their branches and obturator nerve of the hind legs. Clinical signs usually relate to the inability to support weight on the affected limbs due to partial paralysis of the muscles supplied by these nerves, as well as to decreased sensation in the areas of skin supplied by these nerves.

Treatment for these conditions is usually supportive and includes administration of anti-inflammatory medications and glucocorticoids. Good footing, nutrition, hydration, and stall care are important. The effects of prolonged recumbency can be minimized by appropriate positioning during anesthesia and the use of well-padded table surfaces. Recumbent animals also need well-padded surfaces and frequent turning to minimize trauma and compression. A recumbent horse may need assistance in evacuating its rectum of feces and in urinating, requiring manual evacuation of feces and placement of a Foley catheter into the bladder. Some intensive-care hospitals or clever engineering may provide the use of a sling to assist recumbent animals to their feet. The use of a sling can be attempted with regularity to allow for relief of persistent compression of muscle and nerves due to recumbency. Gradually lowering the sling in successive standing attempts allows slung horses to slowly resume standing on their own. However, slings can be dangerous to the horse as well as to its handlers, and not all horses tolerate a sling.

In general, the longer the animal remains recumbent, the more severe the damage is likely to be to the muscle and nerves supplying the muscle. Therefore, the likelihood of regaining the ability to stand decreases with prolonged recumbency. Long-term recumbency without successful attempts at standing is grounds for the consideration of euthanasia.

Behavioral Abnormalities

Behavioral abnormalities that are unrelated to specific diseases have been documented in horses with some frequency. Some such behavior abnormalities are stall-walking, weaving, cribbing, shying, running a fence line, "track sour" behavior, self-mutilation, savagery of other horses or of people, foal rejection, and sexual-behavior dysfunction in breeding stallions.

Many behavior abnormalities that are not associated with a diagnosed disease process are likely to be learned behaviors — perhaps acquired to combat boredom. The neural pathways involved could stimulate the release of certain chemicals in the central nervous system that promote the repetition of the behavior.

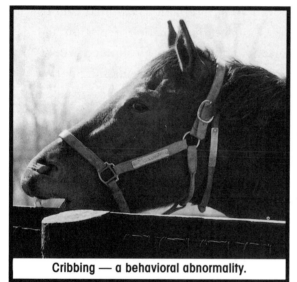

Cribbing — a behavioral abnormality.

Behavioral abnormalities that are caused by organic diseases may affect the cerebrum, the limbic system, or other brain centers. Behavioral changes due to specific diseases require primary treatment of the disease process. The prognosis with such treatment depends on the disease and its severity.

Some of the behavior problems listed above may well be manageable. The owner or handler may need to think of creative ways to keep the horse occupied and interested in its surroundings. For example, a horse that weaves or stall-walks may respond to the presence of a stall toy, a companion, or other changes in its environment or routine.

Some behavioral abnormalities may be associated with actual imbalances of chemical messengers in the central nervous system or with other neurological problems.

Diagnosis and treatment of such problems may not be simple. These conditions may require evaluation and treatment by an animal behaviorist to maximize the likelihood of success in treatment and management. Behavioral abnormalities such as savagery and self-mutilation may require consideration of euthanasia on the grounds of safety and humaneness.

CHAPTER 12

Management of the Neurologically Impaired Horse

NONSPECIFIC THERAPIES

Several treatments are universally or nearly universally used to treat nervous-system disorders and are not specific to any one disease.

Glucocorticoids ("steroids") (dexamethasone, prednisone, etc.) are used for their powerful anti-inflammatory properties and in instances of immune-mediated disease for their immunosuppressive properties.

Nonsteroidal anti-inflammatory drugs (NSAIDs) (phenylbutazone, flunixin meglumine, ketoprofen, etc.) are used for their anti-inflammatory properties and to relieve pain.

Dimethylsulfoxide (DMSO) is used for its presumed free-radical-scavenging properties and for its anti-inflammatory and diuretic properties (to remove fluid and edema).

Vitamin E is used as an antioxidant in diseased and healthy horses alike to promote and maintain nervous-system health.

Anti-edema (anti-swelling) medications (mannitol, furosemide [Lasix]) are used to control or eliminate edema formation in the nervous system.

SPECIFIC THERAPIES

Specific therapies often are used in conjunction with nonspecific treatments and are targeted at specific disease processes.

Antimicrobials are used against specific bacteria or other organisms, such as protozoa, in the treatment of equine protozoal myeloencephalitis.

Antitoxins are used to neutralize circulating and unbound toxins, such as in cases of tetanus and botulism.

Antidotes are used in specific intoxications to counteract or neutralize the effects of the toxin.

> ## AT A GLANCE
>
> • A variety of treatments are available for nervous-system disorders, from anti-inflammatory medications to therapies such as acupuncture and chiropractic.
>
> • Neurologically impaired horses require special care.
>
> • Advances in diagnostic imaging will aid researchers in diagnosing and treating neurological disorders.

Anti-seizure medications (diazepam [Valium], phenobarbital, phenytoin) are used to control the severity and frequency of seizures.

OTHER THERAPIES

Generally speaking, whenever a preponderance of medications being used for treatment fall under the "other therapies" category, it is safe to surmise that little is known about the disease process(es) being addressed. Therefore, it would not be inaccurate to conclude that our understanding of equine nervous-system diseases and their treatment and management is far from complete. Some of the following therapies may be more useful than others, but all have been investigated thoroughly or at least used extensively, with either written or anecdotal reports of success. They are also the treatments that have the most solid physiologic basis.

Acupuncture

There is no real and repeatable evidence that this modality can be used to treat nervous-system abnormalities. It may,

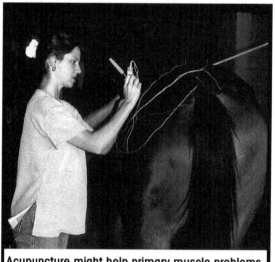
Acupuncture might help primary muscle problems.

however, be useful in addressing either primary muscle problems or muscle problems associated with an underlying nervous-system abnormality.

Chiropractic therapy

Chiropractic is receiving more attention as a useful treatment modality. It may prove to be significantly useful in the treatment of back and neck musculoskeletal pain. Skillful practitioners may be very helpful to the treatment process. Chiropractic therapy still needs to be rigorously and scientifically evaluated in terms of its effects in relation to the nervous system and to nervous-system disorders.

Other Medications

Medications in this category are generally undefined in terms of their clinical effect in the treatment of nervous-system disorders. Some of these medications include infrequently used antimicrobial agents for specific disease processes. Examples of this include oxytetracycline and doxycycline (used to treat EPM). Anti-inflammatory agents in this category include the 21-aminosteroids (a type of drug), such as tirilizad mesylate.

Supplements

Both herbal and non-herbal supplements have been used to support horses with nervous-system derangements. Their use is generally undefined in terms of their efficacy, but they are usually not harmful when administered properly.

PROGNOSIS

The prognosis for any horse with neurologic disease depends on several factors, including the severity, duration, and specific diagnosis of the disease process. As the descriptions of several of the nervous-system diseases described in this book have made clear, some diseases are much more amenable to treatment than are others. Regardless, the prognosis for each horse should be evaluated on a case-by-case basis. General prognoses for specific disease conditions exist, but more specific prognostication should be left to the examining and treating veterinarian.

In general, a horse with nervous-system disease that loses its ability to stand has at best a guarded prognosis. The longer a horse remains recumbent, the worse the prognosis becomes because of the resulting muscle and nerve damage.

CARE OF THE NEUROLOGIC HORSE

The neurologically impaired horse requires special care to help it move and function safely and comfortably. Some horses that are successfully treated may be capable of returning to their previous athletic or other use.

One significant consideration in the care of the neurologically impaired horse involves the decision as to whether the horse can be ridden again. Even in cases of apparent full recovery from nervous-system problems, such horses still pose a significant risk to their riders. Veterinarians should discuss the risks thoroughly with owners of neurologically impaired horses so that their clients understand the safety issues and develop realistic performance expectations. In many cases, the veterinarian may well discourage all riding. A horse may experience no nervous-system problems as the result of tripping or falling, but such an incident could be more dangerous if the horse has recovered from a neurological condition, as it may be more likely for horses to fall and injure themselves and their riders.

Good footing is a must for horses with nervous-system impairment. Footing may be less of a concern if the horse has recovered from a peripheral nervous-system problem, as such problems tend to affect fewer nerves and muscles.

A neurologically impaired horse should be handled with extra care. Handlers should be alert to such possibilities as the horse's falling over or experiencing changes in behavior or senses such as vision or hearing.

If a horse has cranial-nerve deficits, its ability to select, chew, or swallow food may be impaired. Such situations may require special methods of feeding. Horses in pain should have their food and water placed such that eating and drinking causes minimal discomfort.

The administration of medications to horses with nervous-system impairment may require diligent adherence to dosing protocols. Unfortunately, some medications may be required for long periods of time. It is important that medications be administered as directed by the veterinarian to prevent failure of treatment or worsening of the condition.

A horse with nervous-system impairment must be evaluated periodically by a veterinarian. Some cases of nervous-system impairment may worsen even after an apparent period of stability. A good relationship with and periodic evaluation by your veterinarian are important in managing such a situation.

CARE OF THE SEVERELY NEUROLOGIC HORSE

Severely neurologic horses are difficult to manage in a field or even in the stable. They can be dangerous to themselves, to other horses, and to their handlers. A severely affected horse that is able to stand is prone to falling over. A horse with moderate to severe nervous-system impairment should not be ridden under any circumstances. Significant caution must be exercised by experienced handlers when working around such horses.

Recumbent horses are also dangerous. Many horses that become unable to rise will thrash with their legs, head, and neck, posing serious danger to themselves and to others. Seizing horses are even more dangerous, as the thrashing is usually more violent and uncontrollable. A recumbent horse needs heavy, soft bedding and frequent turning from side to side to minimize muscle and nerve damage. Keeping such a horse in a sternal position also is helpful. The use of soft, protective headgear can help minimize trauma and swelling of the head and other areas. Recumbent horses also may experience swollen, abraded eyelids and even corneal ulcers, which must be treated with eye ointments.

A sling is a valuable aid in trying to help a recumbent horse to its feet but is potentially very dangerous. Many — if not most — horses frantically throw their legs in attempts to try to stand or in resistance to being lifted. For this reason, not all horses will be able to benefit by placement in a sling. Some horses may thrash so frantically that they incur more trauma or even suffer a fracture. It takes a skilled team, a cooperative horse, and sometimes mild sedation to maximize the use of a sling.

Feeding and medications are important in managing severely neurologic horses, and special diets or management practices may be necessary. Your veterinarian can help devise an appropriate feeding program.

The overall prognosis of a recumbent horse deteriorates with the time it spends down and unable to rise. In the case of a horse that is able to stand and walk but that has severe nervous-system deficits, it is realistic to expect that its life span will be severely curtailed, regardless of its age. Most horses live only a few more years before falling again, perhaps in the field, and becoming unable to rise. It is appropriate to strongly consider euthanasia in such cases, especially if the horse has required a sling to recover from recumbency in the past.

NEUROLOGIC DISORDERS AND PERFORMANCE

Some neurologic conditions cannot be definitively diagnosed ante-mortem (before death) and are diagnosed by exclusion of other disease processes. These nervous-system conditions are unfortunately often used to explain many conditions and poor performance. The diagnosis of diseases based only on ambiguous signs and incomplete diagnostics leads to overtreatment of nonexistent diseases, a waste of horse owners' money, and clients' dissatisfaction with treatment results. Although there is no way of reaching definitive ante-mortem diagnosis on

The most reliable diagnosis is based on a thorough diagnostic work-up.

some nervous-system disease, the most reliable diagnosis is based on an informed and well-planned diagnostic work-up.

Many neurologically impaired horses suffer from age-related changes in performance or degenerative musculoskeletal conditions. Rest alone occasionally produces some improvement in performance, but often the treatments being administered receive the credit. With good veterinary assistance, chronic degenerative or age-related conditions can be managed in ways that maximize the horse's potential. Therefore, an important part of every neurologic evaluation of a performance horse is a comprehensive lameness and musculoskeletal examination by an experienced veterinarian.

THE FUTURE OF EQUINE NEUROLOGY

Our knowledge of equine neurology is limited and in its infancy. It pales in comparison to the understanding of the human nervous system. Of course, a major impediment to the neurologic evaluation of an animal is the animal's inability to communicate precisely what and how it is feeling. More complete physical and neurologic examinations can be performed on small animals, thanks to their size. For these reasons, equine neurologic evaluations rely more heavily on diagnostic testing and imaging in association with the neurologic examination.

New tests for specific diseases are in development. As researchers learn more about bioengineering, genetics, and DNA, some conditions may become identifiable and perhaps even treatable using molecular genetics and molecular biology.

The real future of equine-neurology research may be in diagnostic imaging. CT and MRI modalities have already been used on foals and may be available in the future for adult horses. Such modalities will enable clinicians to identify the specific locations and even the specific causes of nervous-system abnormalities. Such diagnostic and imaging techniques are likely to remove at least some of the subjectivity from the equine neurologic evaluation and to lead to methods of diagnosing and treating diseases that cannot presently be definitively diagnosed ante-mortem. Such improvements are likely to significantly curtail wasted expenditure and to dramatically enhance therapeutic options and their successes.

Abiotrophy — Failure of normal development.

Acute and convalescent titers — Blood antibody levels drawn in the beginning of disease and several weeks thereafter to detect immune system response to an organism.

Anaerobic — Absence of oxygen.

Ante-mortem — Before death.

Ataxia — Poorly coordinated gait, as if drunk.

Atrophy — Loss in organ size.

Atropine — Drug with effects that block the parasympathetic nervous system.

Borellia burgdorferi — The organism that causes Lyme disease.

Brachial plexus — A nest of peripheral nerves that join together in a complex as they exit the spinal cord and that supply the nerves to the forelimbs.

Brainstem — Base of brain; many cranial nerves exit here.

Cataplexy — Acute loss of muscle strength leading to falling.

Central nervous system — The brain and spinal cord.

Cerebellum — Large sphere behind the cerebrum responsible for coordination of movement and body posture.

Cerebrum — Part of the brain responsible for complex movements and thought.

Cervical spinal column — Spinal column in the neck.

Chelation — Binding of an element to a molecule to facilitate its removal from the body.

Cisterna magna — Space behind the skull from which spinal fluid is collected when the horse is under general anesthesia.

Clostridium botulinum — Organism that makes the toxin that causes botulism.

Clostridium tetani — Organism that makes the toxin that causes tetanus.

Colostrum — First milk containing high levels of antibodies for the foal.

Cranial nerves — Twelve major nerves supplying the head and upper neck and shoulder muscles, some of which are responsible for special senses and involuntary reflexes.

Dermal — Referring to the skin.

Diuretic — Causing excess fluid loss through urination.

Dysphagia — Difficulty in swallowing.

Edema — Fluid swelling.

Electromyography (EMG) — Electrical testing of the nervous input to a muscle.

Electroretinography — Electrical testing of the function of the retina in the eye.

Emboli — Blood-borne material that can cause necrosis when it obstructs a vessel.

Eustachian tube — Ear tube from the throat to the middle ear.

Extracellular fluid — Fluid outside of cells; includes blood and tissue fluid.

GABA — Stimulatory nervous system chemical messenger.

Granuloma — A chronic inflammatory mass that may harbor an infectious agent.

Herniate — Pushed through a space of tissue, often causing pressure and inflammation of the herniated tissue.

Heterozygous — Two different genetic signals for a particular gene, e.g., one dominant, one recessive.

Homozygous — Two identical genetic signals for a particular gene, e.g., two dominant or two recessive.

Horner's syndrome — The syndrome of a drooping eyelid, pupillary constriction, inward setting of the eyeball, protrusion of the third eyelid, increased facial temperature, and sweating on the same side.

Hypoglycemia — Low blood sugar.

Immune-mediated — Caused by reaction of the immune system.

Incontinence — Leaking of urine between periods of active urination.

Intracellular fluid — Fluid inside of cells.

Involuntary nervous system — Automatic nervous system; does not require thought to stimulate.

Ionized — Exists in a charged form.

Limb placement tests — Tests of limb correction after a limb is moved into abnormal locations.

Lumbosacral space — Space over the pelvis over which the "hunter's bump" is located; spinal fluid collection site in the standing horse.

Luxation — Malalignment of bones of a joint.

Lymphosarcoma — Cancer of the lymphatic system; spreads easily.

Lysis — Breakage.

Medulla — Uppermost portion of the spinal cord.

Meningitis — Inflammation of the tissue layers covering the central nervous system.

Motor fiber — A nerve fiber that sends information to the body by way of motor nerve tracts to cause movement or other effects in the organ to which it courses.

Myelin — Substance that forms a sheath around the processes of nerve cells.

Myelography — Contrast dye injected into the space around the spinal cord and X-rays taken to detect areas of spinal cord compression.

Necrosis — Tissue death usually due to loss of blood supply.

Neuroborreliosis — Nervous system disease caused by *Borellia burgdorferi*.

Nuclear scintigraphy — Injection of radioactive substance that is taken up by inflamed areas of soft tissue and bone. Detected by a gamma camera.

Nystagmus — Rhythmical movements of the eyes associated with vestibular or cerebellar disease.

Oxygen-derived free radicals — By-products of immune cell metabolism that are destructive to tissue.

Panniculus reflex — Skin twitch response to poking or other skin stimulus.

Parasite — Foreign organism that feeds off of the host's body systems.

Parasympathetic nervous system — Portion of the involuntary nervous system that generally counteracts.

Perineum — Skin around the anus.

Peripheral nervous system — Nerves that branch out from the central nervous system.

Positive predictive value — Likelihood that a positive test represents a truly diseased animal.

Post-mortem — After death.

Proprioceptive deficits — Loss of the ability to detect the limbs in space.

Pupillary light reflex — Response of the pupils to light by constriction.

Reflexes — Automatic responses to certain stimuli.

Sarcocystis neurona — Major protozoa causing EPM.

Segmental reflexes — Reflexes relating to each segment of the spinal cord and spinal column.

Sensory fiber — A nerve fiber that sends sensory information from the body to the brain in sensory nerve tracts in the spinal cord.

Septicemia — Bacteria and its toxins within the blood.

Slap test — Movement of the arytenoid cartilage of the hyoid apparatus in response to a slap on the withers on the opposite side.

Spinal fluid analysis — Analysis of many types possible on the spinal fluid (cell counts, bacteria, antibody detection, protein amounts, culture).

Stylohyoid bone — Bone of the hyoid apparatus involved in swallowing and vocalizing.

Symmetry/asymmetry — Relating to similar findings on both sides of body (symmetric) or dissimilar findings on the sides of the body (asymmetric).

Sympathetic nervous system — Portion of the involuntary nervous system generally responsible for automatic stimulatory responses.

Thiamine — Vitamin B1.

Thumps — Synchronous diaphragmatic flutter; simultaneous contraction of the heart and diaphragm muscle.

Tracheostomy — Temporary surgical hole in the trachea.

Tympanic bulla — Bony cavity on the underside of the skull that communicates with the middle ear.

Vasculitis — Inflammation of a blood vessel.

Vertebrae — Bones of the spinal column.

Vestibular — Referring to the inner ear structures responsible for balance and sensation of motion.

Viscera — Referring to the organs of the body.

Voluntary nervous system — Nervous system requiring conscious decisions to stimulate.

INDEX

Andrews FM, Fenner WR. Indications and Use of Electrodiagnostic Aids in Neurologic Disease. Veterinary Clinics of North America: Equine Practice. 1987. 3(2): 293-322.

Ansari MM, Matros LE. Tetanus. Compendium on Continuing Education for the Practicing Veterinarian. 1982. 4(11): S473-S478.

Beech J. Neuroaxonal dystrophy of the Accessory Cuneate Nucleus in Horses. Veterinary Pathology. 1984. 21: 384-393.

Bentz BG, Ross MR. Otitis Media/Interna in Horses. Compendium on Continuing Education for the Practicing Veterinarian. 1997. 19(4): 524-533.

Bentz BG, Carter WG, Tobin T. Equine Protozoal Myeloencephalitis: Diagnostic Complications. Compendium on Continuing Education for the Practicing Veterinarian. 1999: 21(10): 975-981.

Blythe LL, Craig AM. Equine Degenerative Myeloencephalopathy. Part I. Clinical Signs and Pathogenesis. Compendium on Continuing Education for the Practicing Veterinarian. 1992. 14(9): 1215-1221.

Blythe LL, Craig AM. Equine Degenerative Myeloencephalopathy. Part II. Diagnosis and Treatment. Compendium on Continuing Education for the Practicing Veterinarian. 1992. 14(12): 1633-1636.

Cauvin E, Munroe GA, Mitsopolous A. Peripheral neuropathy involving brachial plexus nerves in TWO horses. Equine Veterinary Education. 1993. 5(2): 90-94.

Divers TJ, de Lahunta A, Summers BA, Mohammed HO, Valentine BA, Cooper BJ, Cummings JF. Equine Motor Neuron Disease: A New Cause of Weakness, Trembling, and Weight Loss. Compendium on Continuing Education for the Practicing Veterinarian. 1992. 14(9): 1222-1226.

Firth EC. Horner's Syndrome in the Horse: Experimental Induction and a Case Report. Equine Veterinary Journal. 1978. 10(1): 9-13.

Freeman DE. Diagnosis and Treatment of Diseases of the Guttural Pouch (Part I). Compendium on Continuing Education for the Practicing Veterinarian. 1980. 2(1): S3-S11.

Freeman DE. Diagnosis and Treatment of Diseases of the Guttural Pouch (Part II). Compendium on Continuing Education for the Practicing Veterinarian. 1980. 2(2): S25-S31.

Green SL, Smith LL, Vernau W, Beacock SM. Rabies in horses: 21 cases (1970-1990). Journal of the American Veterinary Medical Association. 1992. 200(8): 1133-1137.

Green SL, Little CB, Baird JD, Tremblay RRM, Smith-Maxie LL. Tetanus in the Horse: A Review of 20 Cases (1970-1990). Journal of Veterinary Internal Medicine. 1994. 8(2): 128-132.

Jackson CA, deLahunta A, Dykes NL, Divers TJ. Neurological manifestation of cholesterinic granulomas in three horses. Veterinary Record. 1994. 135: 228-230.

Lester G. Parasitic Encephalomyelitis in Horses. Continuing Education for the Practicing Veterinarian. 1992. 14(12): 1624-1630.

Little CB, Hilbert BJ, McGill CA. A retrospective study of head fractures in 21 horses. Australian Veterinary Journal. 1985. 62(3): 89-91.

Mayhew, IG. Milne Lecture: The Equine Spinal Cord in Health and Disease; Part I: The Healthy Spinal Cord. Proceedings American Association of Equine Practitioners. Albuquerque, NM. 1999: 56-66.

Mayhew, IG. Milne Lecture: The Equine Spinal Cord in Health and Disease; Part II: The Diseased Spinal Cord. Proceedings American Association of Equine Practitioners. Albuquerque, NM. 1999: 67-84.

Mayhew IG. Measurements of the Accuracy of Clinical Diagnoses of Equine Neurologic Disease. Journal of Veterinary Internal Medicine. 1991. 5(6). 332-335.

Mayhew IG, Donawick WJ, Green SL, Galligan DT, Stanley EK, Osborne J. Diagnosis and prediction of cervical vertebral malformation in Thoroughbred foals based on semi-quantitative radiographic indicators. Equine Veterinary Journal. 1993. 25(5): 435-440.

Mayhew IG. Odds and SODs of equine motor neuron disease. Equine Veterinary Journal. 1994. 26(5):342-343.

Mittel L. Seizures in the Horse. Veterinary Clinics of North America: Equine Practice. 1987. 3(2): 323-332.

Plumlee KH, Galey FD. Neurotoxic Mycotoxins: A Review of Fungal Toxins That Cause Neurological Disease in Large Animals. Journal of Veterinary Internal Medicine. 1994. 8(1): 49-54.

Raphel CF. Brain abscesses in three horses. Journal of the American Veterinary Medical Association. 1982. 180(8): 874-877.

Reed SM, Bayly WM, Traub JL, Gallina A, Miller LM. Ataxia and Paresis in Horses: Differential Diagnosis. Compendium on Continuing Education for the Practicing Veterinarian. 1982. 3(3): 40-50.

Reed SM. Management of Head Trauma in Horses. Compendium on Continuing Education for the Practicing Veterinarian. 1993: 270-273.

Reilly L, Haebecker P, Beech J, Johnston J, Sweeney C, Hamir A. Pituitary abscess and basilar empyema in four horses. Equine Veterinary Journal. 1994. 26(5): 424-426.

Stewart RH, Griffiths JP. Medical Management of Spinal Cord Disease. Veterinary Clinics of North America: Equine Practice. 1987. 3(2): 429-435.

Williams MA. Lightning Strike in Horses. Compendium on Continuing Education for the Practicing Veterinarian. 2000. 22(9): 860-866.

Yvorchuk-St. Jean K. Neuritis of the Cauda Equina. Veterinary Clinics of North America: Equine Practice. 1987. 3(2): 421-427.

Equine Neurology sites on the Internet

Research at Universities:

The Ohio State University:

http://www.prevmed.vet.ohio-state.edu

The University of Kentucky

http://www.uky.edu/Agriculture/VetScience

The University of Florida

http://www.vetmed.ufl.edu

Other Sources:

The Association of Equine Practitioners:
    http://www.aaep.org/

The Horse:Your Guide to Equine Health Care magazine:

    http://www.thehorse.com

Animal Health Trust

    http://www.aht.org.uk

Picture Credits

CHAPTER 2
Anne M. Eberhardt, 14-16, 20; Cheryl Manista, 18.

CHAPTER 4
Cheryl Manista, 27; Dr. Doug Byars, 28; Dr. Philip Johnson, 38.

CHAPTER 5
Anne M. Eberhardt, 42, 44, 48; Dr. Philip Johnson, 43.

CHAPTER 6
Anne M. Eberhardt, 52.

CHAPTER 7
Anne M. Eberhardt, 65-72.

CHAPTER 10
Thomas J. Divers, 88.

CHAPTER 11
Anne M. Eberhardt, 97, 104; Kim and Kari Baker, 102.

CHAPTER 12
Tom Hall, 108; Anne M. Eberhardt, 112.

Editor — Jacqueline Duke
Cover/Book Design — Suzanne Depp
Assistant Editors — Rena Baer, Judy Marchman
Copy editor — Jennifer O. Bryant
Illustrations — Robin Peterson
Cover Photograph — Anne M. Eberhardt

About the Author

Bradford G. Bentz, VMD, MS, is a graduate of the University of Pennsylvania School of Veterinary Medicine. He received a master's degree in veterinary sciences at the University of Kentucky Maxwell H. Gluck Equine Research Center. Bentz, who was born in Germany, is a Diplomate in Large Animal

Bradford G. Bentz

Internal Medicine with the American College of Veterinary Internal Medicine.

Among his post-graduate training positions were a Residency in Large Animal Medicine at the University of Pennsylvania; part-time emergency clinician at both the Delaware Equine Center in Cochranville, Pennsylvania and New Bolton Center at the University of Pennsylvania; and a commission veterinarian for the Kentucky Racing Commission. Bentz has prepared numerous papers for veterinary journals and is an editorial consultant with *Equus* magazine. He also participated in the instructional video "Lameness in the Horse," produced by The Blood-Horse, Inc. *Understanding Equine Neurological Disorders* is his first book.

Bentz has a private equine veterinary practice and also teaches biology at Eastern Kentucky University. He lives in Richmond, Kentucky, with his wife, Patricia, and their son, Ian.